John Mulholland's
STORY OF MAGIC

John Mulholland's
Story of Magic

THE DEVELOPMENT OF THE ART OF ILLUSION
BY THE CIA'S MASTER MAGICIAN

BY JOHN MULHOLLAND
FOREWORD BY BEN ROBINSON

Racehorse Publishing

Racehorse Publishing books may be purchased in bulk at special discounts for sales promotion, corporate gifts, fund-raising, or educational purposes. Special editions can also be created to specifications. For details, contact the Special Sales Department, Skyhorse Publishing, 307 West 36th Street, 11th Floor, New York, NY 10018 or info@skyhorsepublishing.com.

Racehorse Publishing™ is a pending trademark of Skyhorse Publishing, Inc., a Delaware corporation.

Visit our website at www.skyhorsepublishing.com.

10 9 8 7 6 5 4 3 2 1

Library of Congress Cataloging-in-Publication Data is available on file.

Cover design by Michael Short

Print ISBN: 978-1-63158-309-4
Ebook ISBN: 978-1-63158-310-0

Printed in the United States of America

TO *Pauline, my wife,* WHO LOVES MAGIC AND EVEN ONE MAGICIAN.

Contents

FOREWORD BY BEN ROBINSON ....PAGE IX

PART I

THE EARLY MAGIC SHOWS ....PAGE 1

An account of the beginnings of the art of magic and the manner of men its practitioners were.

PART II

AS THE ART ADVANCED ....PAGE 19

What the magicians of other days have done to bring magic to its present development.

PART III

PRESENT-DAY MYSTIFIERS ....PAGE 47

The progress of magic, and the unbelievable dexterity of today's magicians.

FOREWORD
By Ben Robinson

~~~~~~

THE OLD CLICHÉ IS THAT YOU cannot tell a book by its cover. In the case of *John Mulholland's Story of Magic*, the cover tells us plenty, but perhaps does not inspire judgment. The problem with the cover is that you have to know the backstory of the book to even appreciate that it had a cover at all when it was printed in 1935.

The Great Depression had just washed across the globe and the Golden Age of Magic (1880 to 1920) had also taken its last breaths. During this period, theatres were full of patrons who desired (and received) excellent live, surprising entertainment. Most of the artists who appeared in the European one-ring circus, music hall, or American vaudeville were born to their craft, sometimes through ethnic generational training, such as the Yiddish "tummler" —or, one who comically proffers "prizes and surprises." *John Mulholland's Story of Magic* is the rich brew of street, city square, and traveling Eastern European Romany troubadour—performers with the better gimmick (a plural word developed from a sixteenth-century magician's name). Such won larger audiences, farthings, crowns, dollars, and other *baksheesh* put in their humble collection hats. After all, it is called "show *business*."

Mulholland informs us that sometimes early twentieth-century vaudevillian drama went to the sidewalk; big, white (promotional) ambulances were parked near marquees with huge banners on their doors boldly stating:

"IN CASE THE SAW SLIPS—
TONIGHT — KEITH'S THEATRE!
SEE GOLDIN SAW A WOMAN IN HALVES ! ! ! "

Between acts, sometimes the more daring showmen would have a pail of red liquid poured into the gutter precipitously close to where tickets were purchased. Outdoor entertainment, such as Houdini wriggling free of a straitjacket (*"used on the murderously insane!!!"* his posters yelled), and the outdoor cup-and-ball worker had the same intent: get the audience's money. Mulholland shows us when and what happened when magic moved indoors.

"The flickers" born of the Lumiere Brothers in Paris, otherwise known as "the film business," were brought to the world in 1895. Film changed entertainment forever, but film did not immediately challenge live entertainment. (Most professional entertainers at the dawn of film were skeptical of film as entertainment rivaling variety. One non-believer was named Charlie Chaplin.) Film seemed to be a scrapbook recording of who was seen live. And, all of the characters enclosed in *John Mulholland's Story of Magic* merge with the emerging medium of film. France is the main nation where nascent film emerged, as it was the home of Robert-Houdin's *Theatre Fantastiques*, which would later be owned and managed by Georges Melies, the Father of Modern Special Effects in film. Melies was a celebrated magician, and pioneer filmmaker; his biography made by Martin Scorsese as his film *Hugo* (2011).

One French master magician, juggler, and chapeaugrapher (the art of making many hats with one piece of felt), Felicien Trewey, is seen in some of the very first silent films ever recorded. Not only were such master magicians celebrated on stage; now their agility could be seen on film. British pioneer magician John Nevil Maskelyne is shown in a film from 1896 juggling twelve spinning plates. Such images and performances inspired June Barrows Mussey to utilize Mulholland's massive collection and do a "picture book" illustrating the history he loved hearing Mulholland tell, and act out.

By the time June Barrows Mussey got it in his head that he wanted to celebrate his teacher John Mulholland shortly after Houdini's death on Halloween 1926, Mulholland was just returning from a lengthy tour of Eastern Europe. He'd also been to India, gathering material for his second book *Quicker Than The Eye* (1927).

As it happened, history collided with scholarship. The Great Depression surrounded the wheezing of vaudeville as popular entertainment. Finally, by 1935, the rise of sound film and a scholarly magician who could seemingly do anything were brought into the popular firmament of *John Mulholland's Story of Magic*.

Had June Barrows Mussey not idolized John Mulholland (1898-1970), *John Mulholland's Story of Magic* would never have been published. Mussey went on to adopt the *nom de plume* of "Henry Hay" and wrote what is arguably the most successful and influential book on magic of the twentieth century, *The Amateur Magicians Handbook* (1950). "Hay" dedicated that tome to John Mulholland. *John Mulholland's Story of Magic* has a dedicated master-apprentice relationship written between the lines. Only three years after this book came out, Mussey would go on to write and edit a considerable amount of Mulholland's *Beware Familiar Spirits* (1938).

John Mulholland's Story of Magic is slim, the cordial size of a "children's picture book." Yet, it is meant for young adults with serious inquiry. *John Mulholland's Story of Magic* is very clearly the past to current day's prologue of illusion and wonder shown as a multi-million dollar business with epic stage shows such as Las Vegas's Siegfried & Roy and their cast of many white tigers.

But more so, Mulholland and his work are the artistic link between the nineteenth- and twentieth-century practitioners of the psychological art of legerdemain, The Art of Magic, and the detailed inner secrets of the Italian Renaissance "Montimbanco" and the later Southwark Faire "mountebank."

All of these characters—magician, legerdemainist, conjuror, montimbanco, and mountebank— were the predecessors to John Mulholland.

Born in Chicago just prior to the turn of the century, Mulholland came to New York at age two. Despite his controversial father's background, by age ten young Mulholland was involved in the magic arts and would soon befriend the international stars of magic. He had long professional relationships with Houdini, Blackstone, Thurston, Kellar, and the man who ran a buzz saw through his "victim" nightly, Horace Goldin, "The Royal Illusionist." Mulholland shows us where greatness comes from, especially in terms of his teacher John William Sargent. You will meet all of these characters within.

The world of magic as portrayed by this delightful book is a marvelous beginning for anyone who has been bitten by the magic bug. It seems those once bitten are forever infected with the love of magic, illusion, and making an audience marvel and applaud. If lucky, the hobby becomes a part time source of income, and for very few, a profession.

What a profession! In Paris, it is written backstage at the world famous Moulin Rouge:

Dancers are the hardest working
Jugglers are the most talented
Magicians—they're the crazy ones

The author of the statement is unknown, but surely it was someone who trod those venerable boards in the 1880s. The statement has followed each person who has passed by in over 125 years. The point is that the book you now hold, and will soon delight in, is a panorama of personalities, both sane and not, who thought of the impossible, and then set out to do it. The Moulin Rouge was just one place where magicians hung their hats. Could this savvy quote have been written about Bautier de Kolta, who adorns the early pages in an elegant portrait? DeKolta was famous for making his wife disappear while she sat in a chair center stage. As well, he often sported three suit jackets when walking about; eccentric was he.

Doing the impossible was all in a day's work for June Barrows Mussey and his small publishing house at his home at 66 Fifth Avenue on the northern cusp of the arch bordering Washington Square Park and Greenwich Village. No doubt some of the benches near Mussey's home were soon filled with people looking for a bed once the Depression came crashing. During these harrowing times, Mulholland sought to inspire and entertain with charming history lessons; that is what fueled *John Mulholland's Story of Magic*. (His talents were finely honed as a former Horace Mann instructor.)

Mussey accompanied Mulholland to many of his "lecture-performances." Appearing mostly for private groups (schools, societies), where these history lessons were born, Mulholland spoke of long gone magicians, then duplicated their wonders for his paying audiences. Mulholland is largely credited for inventing the "lecture-platform-performance." It might seem odd to the modern reader that historical education was once a newborn as "entertainment." John Mulholland refined what his teacher John William Sargent had created. Mulholland was quickly contracted to appear by the Fifth Avenue agent William B. Feakins and toured nationally for over forty years with six different programs all based in entertaining history lessons.

While working with his student Mussey, Mulholland lived on Manhattan's Upper West Side, but had an office on 42nd Street in the Times Square area. Mulholland was a first class society performer, and a world-renowned scholar on the history and psychology of the magic arts. Robert Lund, who founded the American Museum of Magic in Marshall, Michigan, wrote of Mulholland, "We have no modern counterpart." Lund referred to Mulholland's ambassadorial countenance, and his many hands-on talents. When the conjuring magazine *Genii* feted Mulholland two years before his death, it took six editors to each address one area of Mulholland's interests, from collecting arcane books (some from the 1300s) or his newest book from the esteemed Scribner, explaining intricacies of Parlour entertaining.

Lest the reader think that "Parlour entertainment" is in some way old fashioned (read "antiquated and not relevant to modern day"), please reconsider.

The world described by Mulholland and Mussey in this story is one of men and women who all learned their craft first for friends, for being the life of the party. This happened well before amateur tricksters ever stepped on stage to learn what perform-ing "magic" was. Hence, the world you will soon delight in is one John Mulholland knew well.

The difficulty many years later lies in seeing this work for what it was at the time of its release. Just as the twenty-first century makes its way to being a paperless society, those in the 1930s flirted with this idea too—out of necessity. Having endured a World War, the invention of the motion picture, telephone, steam engine, and automobile in the same years as the Golden Age of Magic, Mulholland lived through extreme change.

Therefore, in 1935, there were shortages of many goods and money could not be spent on non-essentials, such as, book covers.

Mulholland was impressed that his student, sometime scribe, and librarian was now beginning a publishing business, having somehow also scraped together enough money to attract the most respected American historian, Henry Steele Commager. However those who live for the written word, often create more red ink than black. The book they discussed, Mussey thought, would *not* have a dust jacket. Mulholland was in a delicate position when this book came out.

Houdini had recently died. Many were scrambling to attain his theatrical mantle. The tatters of the World War were still felt. And, a man in Germany was beginning to draw notice for his Worker's Party. Mulholland, fresh from an assignment with the Romanian Secret Service (begun years before), was also just made the full time editor of *The Sphinx* magazine. The scholar-performer Mulholland was busy in a chaotic world.

If you read the final chapter of the book carefully, you will see that Mussey surprised Mulholland by including him in the overall parade.

However, never to be one-upped by his student, Mulholland, unbeknownst to Mussey, had designed the book cover and had a limited amount printed. Few originals survive and this cover is actually thought to be *more valuable* than the book itself. And it exists only because Mulholland would not let out a product under his own name without being "properly dressed."

Mulholland scholars know that the dust jacket to *John Mulholland's Story of Magic* is essentially the magician's brochure for society shows such as at the esteemed NY Junior League (where he entertained royalty with diamonds). Hence, we can see with historical hindsight, this accurate time capsule was finished with élan and cleverness that the world recognized for over forty years. John Mulholland was undeniably the "go to" man for all things magic. (Later in life, Mulholland's cleverness was employed by the CIA—as their first consulting magician.[1])

Let this book warm you to an age where it was not just Douglas Fairbanks's milque-toast character in the epic *The Mark of Zorro* (1920), saying "Hey, have you seen this one?" to introduce a small conjuration. Many of the men and women within these pages often made an unexpected handkerchief suddenly twirl like a skillful ballerina.

Make no mistake, magic is power. Artists who charm become immortal in the repeated tales of their great performance. This story is one man's journey through history. John Mulholland, the artist of illusion and the chain-smoking writer, is a very important magic's beginnings as an art. Mulholland guides us through the societal acceptance of those who offer magic, illusion, and feel-good surprise as pure entertainment. That's a big step from "Pronounced spectre, dark Evil One He! Banish O'devils sin! Flames agulf Now dark O'her!" wrote Reverend Jonathan Pritchard at the Salem witch trials of 1693.

This story is exciting, unusual, and offbeat. Magicians may die, but magic is eternal.

The world *John Mulholland's Story of Magic* points to is still present. This world will impress you, just as it impressed readers when this important book first appeared.

---

1   See: Robinson, Ben, *The MagiCIAn: JohnMulholland's Secret Life*, Lybrary.com, 2nd edition, 2010.

The Early Magic Shows

THERE HAS ALWAYS BEEN MAGIC ever since there have been people with minds to be fooled. But the real early magic was mixed with the work of priestcraft and the medicine men. It was shown to make the impressed spectators give power to the performer.

The magic we know today began but a comparatively short while ago; only a thousand years or so. The entire purpose of this magic is to entertain the spectators. As it has been said about drama that "No play is a play until it is acted," so it is true that magic does not exist except as the performer shows it. The real history of magic therefore would be the biographies of its exponents.

At first the magician, the singer, the story-teller, the acrobat, and all the others of the entertainment world gave their shows on the street-corner, or the market-place, of the village or city where they happened to be. This, of course, made it necessary to limit their equipment to the smallest possible amount. The singer would accompany himself on a lute; the story-teller's costume changes would be one or two extra hats. The magician would also limit himself to apparatus he could carry in his pockets or could find or borrow wherever he happened to be.

The early feats of magic were quite simple. A pebble placed on a table and covered with a hat would multiply to two, to four, to six pebbles. A coin borrowed from a trusting spectator would disappear, to be found later in a cabbage-head taken from the market-basket of another spectator. A borrowed ring would be strung on a man's garter-string, and yet could be whisked off and back on again at pleasure.

Various old story-writers mentioned the performances of magicians in their books, although few even attempted to offer explanations. Were it not for the fact that by word of mouth magicians passed on their tricks through the centuries no one would know how these ancient feats were accomplished. The first printed book explaining this early magic was written in 1584, and while many of the tricks described are still performed, others have passed out of the repertoire of present-day magicians. For instance, to throw a piece of money into a deep pond, "and to fetch it again from whence you list," was dropped when magicians stopped giving their shows out of doors. The ancient performer also mystified the "lookers on" with feats with whipcord, and corn, and borrowed chickens, and other things the spectators of today are not apt to have with them.

Although the tricks were simple the presentation was usually superb. The way magic is shown rather than the way it is done makes it good or bad. A survivor of this old magic was a man who knew but one trick, but presented it perfectly. This street-corner performer had piles of soap and cardboard boxes. He would open a box, drop in a coin and a cake of soap, and close the box. Sometimes the coin would be a gold piece, sometimes a half-dollar or a dime; sometimes only a penny. He put the closed cardboard boxes in a small leather traveling bag hung around his neck. For twenty-five cents one could buy any box in the trickster's bag. No matter which box one chose it would contain a cake of soap—and a penny. The great Houdini told me he watched him for hours, and bought a quantity of soap, but he never caught the man substituting one coin for another.

Of these early magicians we know but little. Of course we know the names of Kingsfield, and Claruis, and many others. We know the feats they showed, but we don't know the order in which they showed them. We know that few ever made more than a bare living, and that they led a roving gypsy life.

It is not known who the man was who is shown in the picture entertaining a group in front of the fountain. He was known only as "The magician of the Château d'Eau," and could be found every clear day for many years at the same spot. He must have been quite good, or he would not have been able to come back day after day to the same place.

It will be noticed that he is wearing a sort of apron. Most of the early mystifiers wore these aprons, which were really only large pockets tied around the waist. These pocket-aprons were so commonly used that even today in Germany the word for magicians is "pocket-players." The old magician carried his few magic properties in this pocket, and was continually taking tricks out of it or putting them back in. As the magicians developed better technique they discarded the aprons. They haven't been used for about a hundred and fifty years.

The pocket-aprons had been discarded by the majority of performers by the time magicians thought about noting in books the methods of doing their magic. It must be remembered that only the more advanced magicians had education and knowledge enough to write books. Probably the only book in which the author advocated using the pocket-apron was printed in 1733, in Spain, which leads us to assume that the mystifiers of that country were the last to discard the aprons. There is no record of anyone in America who used the apron, but in this country men did not usually wear trade uniforms. In old Europe the peculiar form of the magician's apron marked him as other styles of apron marked the cobbler and baker.

When the old European cities began to spread beyond the confines of fortifications, the various trades remained each in its particular section. In one part of town could be found the jewelers, in another the cabinet-makers, and in still another the tin-smiths. Likewise, the street magicians found it better to pick one place to perform, so that those who liked magic would always know where to find it. In several European cities the early maps show where the street wizards used to peddle their mysteries, and it was not uncommon for these streets to be called by some appropriate name, such as, "The Street of Conjurors."

At these street performances the spectators were all so close to the magician that everyone could easily see all the magic even though it was done with small objects. But the more entertaining and skilful men began to attract such large crowds that those in the back saw nothing of the performance. This gradually changed the character of magic performances, and therefore it became necessary to do magic which could be seen by large crowds. The more inventive men began to devise tricks which could be shown to groups of any size. And then having enlarged the scope of their magic, they naturally looked for even larger audiences. Some ingenious fellow thought of showing in large barns. Instead of giving daily shows on a street-corner, the magician would hire a barn, and entertain all the townspeople at once. And rather than attract small group after small group by tooting a trumpet, he would walk about the town announcing again and again that this evening in the big barn would be given a show of mysteries which would "amaze and astonish the beholders."

Among the larger effects developed were: "to break any number of eggs into a hat, and by stirring them with a wand [often called a metempsychostical stick] transform them to pan-cakes, without the aid of fire, leaving the hat unsullied. To light a candle with the point of a sword. To fire a lady's ring from a gun in such a manner, that the same will be found confined in a box under lock and key, one of the company taking the key."

In order to make the performance last longer, a barn performer would often do something besides magic. Juggling and ventriloquism were the most likely of the theater arts

for the magician to attempt, although he might also tell stories, or, if he could, sing popular songs. Sometimes, as shown in the picture, he would have assistants — probably members of his own family. In the picture the costumes show that both son and daughter of the magician are ready to perform. The girl is dressed as a dancer, and the boy as a contortionist — a posture-maker as it was then called. One or another also juggled with the ball and plates shown. Besides taking part in the show, both children would help their father collect whatever money could be got out of the spectators. At that time no magicians had thought of charging admission.

The trick of making birds come out of an empty borrowed hat was one of the old favorites which still continues to be popular with both audiences and men of magic. Today, however, it is usual to make a rabbit instead of pigeons appear in the hat. Of course the trick is to get the bird, or rabbit, into the hat without anyone's seeing it done.

The magicians dressed in costumes as unusual as they could devise in order to seem as unlike ordinary people as possible, for magicians then were thought to have some mysterious power. This power to work magic was supposed to be due to some business arrangement with the devil. That is why one of the superstitious spectators in the picture is praying, while another in fear is turning away to leave such an unholy presence. Even today, strange as it may seem, it is possible to find people with the silly belief that no man could perform magic by skill alone, and that all magicians are possessed of supernormal power. In the old days it was thought good business to dress in weird clothes and mumble incomprehensible words to encourage the spectators' belief in the magician's satanic connection. One magician recommended the following: "Droch myroch, and senaroth betu baroch attimaroth, rounsee, farounsee, hey passe passe."

With more equipment, made necessary by larger and more spectacular magic, the magicians found it necessary to travel in wagons instead of walking from town to town with packs on their backs. Once having procured wagons, the magicians tried to avoid using barns. There were two main reasons. First, often no one would rent a barn to a magician; second, the rent of the barn took a large part of the money collected.

Little by little the showmen improved and developed their wagons. Some carried poles and cloths and planks, with which a fairly presentable stage might be made. The magician finding yards of ribbon in the boy's mouth has such a stage. Other wagons were made so that the end would open and steps could be let down to turn the wagon itself into a stage.

In the picture the magician is wearing clothes of a much later date than those shown in the previous pictures. But although magic advanced in the steps set down here, I must also mention that the presentation of magic in its earlier forms continued, and still continues to exist. And though, as will later be described, magic also advanced from the

wagon-stage period, I saw one of the old wagon shows but a few years ago in Germany. It was a cleverly designed wagon, beautifully made of fine wood. It was large, and drawn by four horses. When the magician found the spot where he chose to give his show, the horses would be unhitched and tied out to graze, and the magician would unfold his stage. Two large doors opened at the end, and swung back out of the way. There in the end of the wagon was a tiny but most attractive stage. Steps were attached so that the magician could leave his stage from time to time to go among his audience; folding chairs, an unbelievable luxury, were brought for the spectators to sit on. The stage was lighted by several specially designed and good-looking lanterns. In short, it was a folding theater on wheels.

Some of the magicians discovered that it was not the size of the apparatus which made an effect in magic suitable for large audiences. This depended rather on whether what was shown could be made interesting. All advances in the art at that time were made by blind experiment. Those ideas which worked were kept, and those which failed were discarded. One of the things discovered was that the more familiar the objects with which the marvels were performed, the more the spectators enjoyed the performance. So it was obvious that if the magicians were to appear before people of society, they must use those objects to which wealthy people were accustomed. Tricks were done with watches, and rings, and playing cards (which were quite costly when printing was first begun, and almost prohibitive in price when made by hand). The magicians also used jewel-cases and snuff-boxes and other costly equipment, and dressed in clothes as fine as any Duke or Earl in their audience.

The magicians who catered to audiences of wealth and title—Fawkes, Breslaw, Katerfelto and Pinetti—sometimes gave their shows in the castles of the nobility or the houses of the merchant princes, and at other times engaged the parlor of the local inn, where they would present their magic nightly at a fixed hour. These men were the first to charge a fixed fee for admission. They also advertised their performances in the newspapers instead of walking about the streets announcing their show. At that time the newspapers circulated largely among the wealthy.

The old woodcut showing the magician in a drawing-room performing before gentlemen of fashion was made in Holland about the time of the Declaration of Independence. It is amusing to notice that he is showing the same feat that the old barn performer exhibited for the country people. His hair is curled in the height of fashion, and his clothes seem quite as good as those of his audience.

It will be remembered that some of the magicians were still performing on street-corners, as some do even today, while others continued to hire barns, and still others had wagon shows. All types of people are amused by magic, and therefore there must be many types of magicians.

A stack of three cups is on the table of the Dutch magician. It is the same trick that the street performer, pictured before, was showing, and is one trick which is still shown

by men of magic all over the world. It was so obviously a good idea for magic that it was invented time and time again. Naturally, when various races each invented it independently, there were slight differences in method; but the effect is always almost the same. Three cups are inverted on a table, and under each is put a ball. Upon the magician's command the balls wander from one cup to another. At one time they are all under one cup; at another, gone altogether; and at still another time the balls have all been transformed into other objects. The Europeans caused the balls to quadruple in size, or more often to become steaming hot roast potatoes. The Egyptians made the balls change into tiny chicks, which as soon as the cup was lifted would cheep-cheep and try to run away. In China the magician uses little mice rather than hot potatoes or baby chickens. Otherwise everything about the trick except the shape of the cups is the same. The shape of the cups is due merely to the difference in tastes of different people; and whether the cups are tapering or straight, of brass, wood, paper, or clay, makes no difference to the audience.

Breslaw was one of the most famous of the old magicians, and the picture of the magician showing a card trick is supposed to be his portrait. The artist intended to burlesque the pictures of the members of the audience in order to depict the amazement with which everyone viewed magic at that time.

Breslaw's name was attached to one of the early books on magic, and we have an exceptional record of the sort of mysteries he performed. The book was called *Breslaw's Last Legacy* and promised on the title page to explain all the various performances of legerdemain, sleight of hand, and transformations. One of his featured mysteries was performed with a small bag of calico, or printed linen. He carefully showed the spectators that the bag was empty. He even turned it wrong side out to convince them. When he turned it right side out again he began, after mumbling a few words supposedly in Latin, to take out egg after egg, which had somehow or other appeared in the bag. After having taken out a dozen eggs or so, Breslaw would turn the bag upside down, and shake out a lively but disgruntled hen.

He had another trick which he described in this modest manner. "It is not one of the worst tricks to burn a thread handsomely, yet to make it whole again and it will seem very strange." Another of his feats was to cut a piece of lace from the ruffle of one of the gentlemen in the audience. "Then with words and fretting it is made whole again. This, if it be well handled will seem miraculous." Again and again he cautions all magicians "not to forget the terms of the art to amaze the beholders." It can be seen therefore that he considered the mumble-jumble words of his talk most important. Among his other effects were "to knit a knot upon a handkerchief and to undo the same with words," and "to make three little figures dance in a glass upon the table."

Not only did Breslaw and those magicians of his time perform their tricks, but they also professed knowledge of subjects which it is improbable they knew anything about. They claimed to be able by pronouncing certain words to cure tooth-ache, to make a cement for mending broken glass, to make a lantern which would enable a person to read by night at a very great distance, and to make a jacket for supporting people in water.

Perhaps the card trick which the artist shows in the picture is the one, a favorite of

Breslaw's, in which a card "any man thinks on is conveyed into the kernel of a nut."

Peeking through the curtain can be seen the magician's assistant. At one time most magicians had these comically dressed clown helpers. The term for such a person was "Merry Andrew." With the exception of one performance in Turkey, I have never seen an assisting Merry Andrew. These clowns used to pretend to be afraid of the magic, and run and hide, to try to discover the method of the trick—which of course they could never do—, to tell jokes, or to do whatever else it might occur to them would amuse the audience. Outside of Turkey, no magician uses a Merry Andrew today.

Abandoning the old attitude that magicians were wicked men who had trafficked with the devil, people began to believe that magic was one of the highest forms of science, making use of all other scientific knowledge. As before when the magicians made capital of the laymen's unfounded belief in the magician's wickedness, so now magicians made use of the new idea of their great wisdom. They changed the talk which accompanied their tricks from the meaningless jargon supposed to be necessary for casting spells to pseudo-scientific phrases equally meaningless.

Not only did they change their patter, which is the name for showmen's speeches, but they took pains to give themselves high-sounding titles. One man announced he had been made a Doctor of Science by all the leading Universities. That is, all the universities except the one near which he was appearing. And it was quite common for a magician to call himself professor. The title of professor for a magician became so expected that I frequently even now am addressed as Professor.

As the magicians claimed to be possessed of extraordinary scientific knowledge they found it profitable to adorn their stages with an accumulation of objects few of which they ever used. They did this partly because it gave one the impression that he had seen but a small part of what the magician was capable of showing, and so would be inclined to come soon again; partly because it fulfilled the then popular idea of what a scientist's laboratory looked like.

Such a cluttered stage is shown in the drawing. The picture is not a portrait of any particular wizard, and was used on the playbills of many. It was common to have a stock picture for advertising magic and magicians, even though the picture had no real connection with the work or appearance of any. The engravings used to print pictures have always been expensive, and it is much cheaper for a number to share one picture.

Usually these pictures are owned by a printer who charges nothing extra for them; in fact he has had them made as an extra inducement in getting the showman's printing business. Of course if a performer is successful enough to afford having his own pictures made, he invariably does so.

BRESLAW'S New CAPITAL PERFORMANCES will
be diſplayed,

AT the Great Room, PANTON STREET.
HAY-MARKET, on MONDAYS, WEDNES-
DAYS, FRIDAYS, and SATURDAYS; and likewiſe
at Mr. Loſt's Great Room, late KING's ARMS TA-
VERN, CORNHILL, on TUESDAYS and THURS-
DAYS, in each place to begin preciſely at ſeven o'clock.

Part I. Mr. Breſlaw will exhibit his new invented Magical
Card Deceptions, Letters, Numbers, Dice, Handkerchiefs,
Rings, Pocket Pieces, &c. &c. and particularly he will com-
municate the thoughts from one perſon to another, without
aſking any queſtions.

Part II. Two Favourite Songs by a Young LADY, and
ſeveral amazing DECEPTIONS by a Pupil of Mr. Breſlaw's.

Part III. The celebrated Miſs ROSOMOND, a Child
about eleven years of age, will deliver a SATYRICAL LEC-
TURE on HEADS, the particulars of which will be ex-
preſſed in the bills.

Part IV. Mr. Breſlaw will diſplay a variety of new Deceptions, with ſix different Metals, Magical Watches, Gold
Boxes, Silver Cup, Caſkets, Glaſs and Silver Machinery,
&c. &c. and particularly with a new grand Apparatus and
Experiments, not to be equalled in Europe.

In each place the doors to be opened at ſix o'clock, and to
begin at ſeven.

The Rooms will be kept warm, and elegantly illuminated.
Admittance Two Shillings each perſon.

Tickets and Places to be taken at the places of performance.

N. B. Any perſon inclinable to learn ſome Deceptions on
reaſonable terms, may apply to Mr. Breſlaw, No. 57, Hay-
market.

This preſent Evening,
At FAWKES's Theatre in Jamer-ſtreet, near
the Hay-market, is to be ſeen the following Entertainments,

1. HIS ſurprizing Tricks by Dexterity of Hand, in which he far exceeds all
that ever perform'd in Europe.

N. B. With ſeveral Curioſities of that Kind entirely
New. In particular, he throws the Cards up, and cauſes any of them to ſtick againſt the Cieling, and the
reſt to fall down. Likewiſe he cauſes the whole Pack
to ſtick up to the Cieling, and calls them down by their
Names, one by one.

2. His famous Poſture-maſter.

3. His Muſical Clock.

4. His Puppet-ſhow, being a Play call'd, The Falſe
Lover; or, The Batchelor's Laſt Shift.

5. A curious Piece of Machinery, repreſenting his ſa-
cred Majeſty King George with the moſt illuſtrious Houſe
of Lords as they ſit in Parliament.

At the particular Deſire of ſeveral Gentlemen and Ladies, for the Benefit of the Famous Poſture-Maſter
Phillips, on Monday next will be preſented their di-
verting Entertainments. And beſides their uſual Performances, Mr. Fawkes and Mr. Phillips will perform
ſeveral Curioſities never ſhewn in London before. Price
2 s. and 1 s.

Note, Our Time of performing in this Place is very
ſhort; and we begin this Evening at Seven o' Clock, and
on Monday at Six.

EARLY MAGICIANS' ANNOUNCEMENTS FROM NEWSPAPERS OF 1727 AND 1782

Mr. WIESS'
GRAND
PERFORMANCE.

Mr. WIESS will bring forward his astonishing Performance, which will consist of a great variety of incomprehensible experiments in **NATURAL PHILOSOPHY** and **APPARENT NECROMANCY**, which, for ingenuity of invention, surpasses any thing of the kind ever exhibited in this Country. It has been the aim of Mr. W. to establish an Entertainment instructive to youth, and gratifying to all. In the course of the evening, a new and rich collection of Apparatus will be introduced.

PART I.

The Evening's amusement will commence with **CARDS, RINGS, WATCHES, MONEY, HANDKERCHIEFS, FRUIT, BOXES, BIRDS, &c.** which will elude the sight of the most attentive observer, being the grandest display of deceptive talents, and unquestionably the rarest piece of Magical ability yet exhibited. As for Cards, he will make them do any thing but speak.

Don Quixotte's Mill.

The Performer will present to the Company, this astonishing Mill, which will go and stop as often as any person may require. This comes as near Perpetual Motion as any thing yet invented.

Mysterious Cylinder, which will appear and disappear
in a wonderful manner.

Coffin of Mahomet,
Or a Lady's Glove turned into a LIVE BIRD.

ART OF CARTOMANCY, VIZ:

Column of Roseback.

This experiment has been considered by all persons who have witnessed it, the *Ne Plus Ultra*, of human skill and dexterity. It is as follows:—A Card being secretly chosen by a Lady or Gentleman present, and returned into the pack, the Performer will, by his address, shoot the identical Card against the Column. This experiment, from its extraordinary character, must be seen to be believed.

PART II.

A LECTURE ON MYSTERIOUS EXPERIMENTS, and MAGICAL DELUSIONS, which will shew the *Invisible Being*, or *Little Courier*, who appears and disappears, and is afterwards found with one of the Spectators. M. W. will swallow several pieces of Money, and cause them to ring in his throat, and they will afterwards be found with one of the Company. He will give a piece of money to a person, who will shut it up closely in his hand, and notwithstanding which, the Piece will disappear in a singular manner.

The Automation Dance, or Astonishing Powers of MAGNETISM.

He will break a number of Gentlemen's Watches, and restore them again. He will cut a Lady's Gown or Handkerchief, and unite them again in such a manner that the most discriminating eye cannot discover the least blemish.

PILLARS of HERCULES.

This apparatus has been the admiration of the most scientific persons of every country. Any number of persons in the company making choice of several Cards from a pack, closely examined, and shuffled into said pack again, by putting them into this mysterious Machinery, each Card so chosen and shuffled, shall, by only mentioning its name, (at the will of the Performer,) jump from the pack to the table.

METAMORPHOSE OF THE WATCH—MAGICIANS CAP—VOLCANIC BOX—MYSTERIOUS EGGS—MAGICAL ALFRIDATE, &c.

THE WONDERFUL FACTORY,
Which has astonished many Philosophers.
He will also perform many curious and amusing tricks, too numerous to mention.

Performance to commence at   o'clock. The Performance will vary every evening. Mr. W. engages to return the money paid for admission to any person, should he feel disappointed with his performance.

☞ N. B. The professor of the above will give lessons to Amateurs, and furnish them with Mechanical and Philosophical Apparatus in his line, on reasonable terms, should any application be made.

Some of the apparatus depicted was actually used in magic. The trick the magician is doing is that of causing a watch and chain, borrowed from one of the spectators, to be discovered in a fresh loaf of bread, after having mysteriously disappeared but a moment before. I performed this trick once, and when the watch was returned to its owner he held it to his ear, and announced to the entire audience as well as to me that the watch was not running. I, of course, was most embarrassed, and told him so. "Oh, that's all right!" said the watch's owner. "I was merely hoping that the magic would make it run, for, you see, it hasn't been going for a week. Guess I'll have to get a watch-maker to work some real magic on it."

As in the previous picture, the one on the next page shows a magician appearing on a stage. At first these stages were built in one end of a store rented for several months as a small theater. As magic became more popular, theater-owners would engage magicians for different seasons of the year, for by this time theaters were growing common. Certain of the more fearless performers even hired the theater themselves, and in that way made—or lost—all the money.

The magician who has such wierd companions as a skeleton and the devil behind the table was named Wiess. He was not very well known, but this picture, which appeared at the top of the announcement of his show, is an excellent example of the extravagant advertising of many of the old magicians. Of course no devil appeared, and the magician was not assisted by a person divested of flesh and skin. It was merely Wiess's fancy that this would attract attention to his announcement, and besides he really did appear to cut off and restore the head of one assistant. Some of my readers may have seen a magician cause a skeleton to appear mysteriously and cavort about the stage as if he had muscles and a brain to make them work; but that is a much later trick.

The feat which he is showing of finding a dove in a bottle is the end of one of the most popular old bits of magic. At the beginning the magician brings forth a tray on which are several wine-glasses and a bottle. The announcement is calmly made that the conjurer will pour from his bottle whatever the audience demands. Red wine, white wine, ale, or whiskey may be called for first. It is immediately poured from the bottle. Some one else asks for one of the other drinks, and it too is poured from the bottle. When the bottle has been emptied the magician suggests that many of those present would undoubtedly like to see inside. He then takes a hammer, smashes the bottle, and

out flies a dove. I first saw this trick done when I was five years old, and even today, having gone all around the world and having seen the best magicians, I still remember it as an exceptional piece of magic.

The decapitation which allows the person to be made whole again the moment the head is replaced goes back to ancient Egypt. One of the most effective bits of this trick is when the detached head calls to the magician, begging him to replace the head before he forgets. Sometimes the magician asks the head if it would like to smoke. Upon being assured that it would, he puts a cigarette between the lips, and gives it a light. The head then smokes, seemingly with complete enjoyment. I have seen this decapitation trick in India. The magician was a street performer, and would not begin until all the bystanders had contributed money. Once the head was severed the magician declared that unless those watching would give more money he wouldn't be bothered with restoring the head. Naturally everyone hurriedly tossed him more money, and the trick was completed, to the satisfaction of the assistant, the audience, and the magician's pocketbook.

Of course no magician ever had a gnome ride a spider across his stage, nor pretend to do so. This and the extra dozen or so rabbits coming out of the hat in the previous picture were put in by the artists for their own amusement.

Although the several steps in the advancement of the art may quickly be described, hundreds of years were necessary for the magicians to bring magic to the point of stage performance. We must remember, too, that not merely the few men I have named made all the progress: thousands of magicians each added to the general knowledge of many new mysteries and a few new methods.

Magicians always agreed with their audiences, although they realized they needed neither devil nor special wisdom, but perfected themselves in their art by years and years of practice. Magicians have always known that they could entertain the spectators as long as they could mystify them.

As the Art Advanced

THE BEGINNING OF THE NINETEENTH CENTURY found magicians going along much as they had been for a hundred years before. It is true that many new bits of magic had been devised, and that the technique of magic was improving, but the changes came slowly. But the early part of the century brought a new kind of magic to Europe and America. It was shown by men from the Orient.

One of the early troupes came from Seringapatam, India, and was headed by Ramo Samee. It played both in England and in the United States. An advertising pamphlet describing its performance mentions several effects new to the Western World. For instance, "The Indian lays upon the palm of his hand a small quantity of sand. This he rubs with the fingers of his other hand, and it changes its hue—the colorless grains become yellow; he rubs them again, they are white; again, and they are black." Or again, "A small quantity of rice in the hands is taken, and by turning it round with a small basket, the quantity is considerably increased, and it soon takes the appearance of having been actually baked on the fire. The rice is shown to the company in both states."

Several Indian magicians had appeared in Europe before the advent of a Chinese mystifier. The magic shown by the first Chinese featured the surprising appearance of a huge bowl of water, or fruit, from the folds of an innocent silk cloth. Another spectacular feat was the linking and disjoining of a number of large solid metal hoops. Together the Indians and the Chinese brought a large variety of novel effects, which we still know: threading small beads on a horsehair in the mouth, sticking swords through a boy in a basket, tearing a strip of paper and making it whole and producing a lighted lantern out of a bowl of water.

The program of one Chinese company headed by Tuck Guy announced "Magic and

Necromancy never performed but in the Celestial Empire. The first night of the aston-ishing feat of the decapitation since their departure from the city of Hongkong where they performed to crowded houses. This great feat is the most daring, expert, and astonishing ever witnessed. The audience need not fear the slightest alarm as no accident can happen."

Of course this new Oriental magic was too good to be overlooked by the magicians of the Western World, but the credit of popularizing it goes to Phillippe, a French magician born in 1802. (He spelled his name with one "l," but it usually appeared in print with two. I use the latter.) He was playing in Dublin at the time of the appearance there of a Chinese troupe, and learned the secrets of Chinese magic from them; from some vis-iting Indian company he later acquired Indian magic. I imagine he traded his tricks for theirs. He thought so much of his new deceptions that he grouped them in a special part of his program which he entitled, "'A Night in the Palace of Peking."

Reading his program and the description of this special act one is apt to decide that he was a little confused in grouping both Indian and Chinese magic in a Peking Palace. As a matter of fact there were few Indian tricks spectacular enough to exhibit on a stage, and he did not use those few—unless they are hidden behind the weird names on the pro-gram. He did feature "The Bowl of Neptune and the Fish," which announced the mysterious appearance of a bowl filled with water and goldfish.

The picture shows him dressed as he imagined a high-class Chinese would dress. His clothes are really a combination of the Chinese and of the old-type conjurers.

Inaccurate as was his dress and confused as were his Oriental and Occidental magic, he performed, as his program said, "The most surprising feats ever attempted by any European." Furthermore he popularized these new additions to the art during his travels throughout Europe and the British Isles.

Remembering that he was a particularly skillful and clever magician, we are amused to know that before he began as a magician he was a candy-maker, and first went with a show the better to peddle his wares.

One of the feats of magic in the European part of Phillippe's program was lighting two hundred and fifty candles by firing a pistol. Many of his other tricks required al-most as great an array of paraphernalia.

The high point in filling the stage with apparatus was reached by John Henry Ander-

son. His program describes his equipment as "of solid silver, the mysterious mechanical construction of which is upon a secret principle hitherto unknown in Europe." Upon his appearance in Boston, however, the newspapers chose to feature his effect of finding his son and a considerable variety of odds and ends all tucked in an empty paper portfolio.

Anderson began touring with shows while still a small boy, first as a circus performer and later as an actor. When he met a magician he decided that this was the branch of stage art he would follow. He had considerable success in his native Scotland and throughout England. He toured America and Australia.

His great contribution to magic was to demonstrate the value of publicity. He was boastful, bombastic, and regularly inaccurate, but he showed magicians the importance of the printed word. He showed, too, the public's interest in stories about the people of the theater. In publicizing himself he left no stone unturned. When he was honored by a command performance before Queen Victoria, he had a medal struck to commemorate the event. It is true that many of those who received copies of the medal believed it had been made by order of the Queen, but Anderson had little judgment in matters of taste. He had an illustrated alphabetical program of his show which he circulated widely to children, knowing that if they became interested they would everlastingly plead to have their parents take them to his show. This book begins, "A is for Anderson's magical name, embodied so fair on the roll call of fame. Made great by the right of his mystical wand, and familiar as famous in every land." The verse is weak, to say the least, but the pictures of all the famous mysteries more than made up for poor versification to the children who got the book. He also published a series of tiny pamphlets for adults describing among other things an adventure supposed to have happened to him in Ireland, and an interview with the Emperor of Russia.

Anderson, by his continual publicity in newspapers, his pamphlets, and by having excellent pictures made not only of himself but of the tricks which he performed, built a reputation quite out of proportion to his skill as a magician. Not that he did not entertain his audiences with his elaborate show, but the majority of even his more skillful rivals were bested by his advertising.

Anderson should receive credit also for his work in disclosing the cheats used by alleged ghost-raisers in preying upon the credulous. Anderson was probably the first magi-

cian who took the trouble to expose these who were using legerdemain to defraud the public.

John Henry Anderson is shown in the picture appearing before a Royal audience at one of his many command performances.

Robert Houdin, at one time a competitor of Anderson, is usually called the father of modern magic. Although he did not invent all of the mysteries he presented, he claimed to have done so. Of course no other magician has ever been able to give a show without

PHILLIPPE'S

SOIREES MYSTERIEUSES.

EVERY EVENING.

Will commence with M. PHILLIPPE'S Celebrated and Unrivalled

TOURS DE PHYSIQUE,

AND ASTOUNDING FEATS OF

MAGICAL DELUSIONS!

Which he has exhibited in Paris, Vienna, Berlin, St. Petersburg, and before all the Courts of Europe, with truly unparalleled success, including his peculiar and unequalled

Metamorphoses and Astonishing Deceptions.

THE MAGIC VASE AND CUPID'S PALACE.

WITH OTHER

STRIKING TRANSFORMATIONS

THE FIRST PART WILL TERMINATE WITH A

Grand Distribution and New Method of Making Coffee,

BETWEEN THE FIRST AND SECOND PART.

THE CHIARINI FAMILY

WILL APPEAR IN A

NEW BALLET DIVERTISSEMENT.

IN WHICH WILL BE INTRODUCED

LA MINUET DE LOUIS XV.

BY LA PETIT CHIARINI.

PART 2,—WILL CONSIST OF

A NIGHT IN THE PALACE OF PEKIN!

In which M. PHILLIPPE will perform some of the most Extraordinary

TOURS D'ADRESSE AND NOVEL EXPERIMENTS, consisting of

| The Turtle Dove and the Flying Handkerchiefs. Endless Profusion. | The Mystic Sugar Loaf. Kitchen of Parahagaramus. |

THE PERFORMANCE TO CONCLUDE WITH M. PHILLIPPE'S MOST BRILLIANT

INDIAN & CHINESE FEATS!

BEING THE MOST SURPRISING WONDERS EVER ATTEMPTED BY ANY EUROPEAN, ENTITLED

LES BASSINS DE NEPTUNE ET LES POISSONS D'OR AND THE GRAND MENAGERIE.

Unanimously pronounced to be the most inexplicable and surprising Tours de Physique ever executed, and which is nightly hailed with Thunders of Applause.

Doors opened at Quarter-past 7, Performance to commence Quarter to 8.

LYCEUM ROYAL THEATRE.

Lessee, Mr. J. H. ANDERSON, Burleigh Street, Strand.

TUESDAY, DECEMBER 11th, 1855,

The Grand ELEUSINIAN SPECTACLE ("Tempore, quo vobis initia est Cerealis Eleusin."—Ov. Ep. 4, 67.) of

MAGIC AND MYSTERY,

In Twelve Acts, with nearly Five Hundred Incidents, by

PROFESSOR ANDERSON

THE GREAT WIZARD OF THE NORTH,

PROGRAMME.—PART 1.

ACT I.

THE MESMERIC COUCH;

Or, the CLINICAL CAPABILITIES of the ATMOSPHERE.

In which the Wizard will do by Magic that which some suppose to be effected by Mesmerism, and illustrate the possibility of Sleeping Unsupported in the Air.

ACT II.

MAGICAL LOCOMOTION;

Or, TRANSITION WITHOUT TROUBLE.

In which will be comprised—The Adventures of a Wedding Ring, The Peregrinations of a Bank Note, The Transformation Black into White, and The Discovery of every Article in the position which would seem the most inappropriate.

ACT III.

L'ECRIN DE VERRE;

Or, THE CASKET OF KING CRŒSUS,

Into which, though made entirely of Glass perfectly transparent, and suspended so as to be visible to the eyes of all present, the Wizard will cause the Money of his Visitors to transport itself and rain into the Casket, though its lid be closed, locked, and the key in the possession of the Audience.

ACT IV.

CLAIRVOYANCE EXTRAORDINARY;

Or, THE TRANSPARENCY OF OPACITY.

ACT V.

THE NEW BOTTLE OF BACCHUS;

Or, THE NOVEL WINE & SPIRIT STORE.

An Improvement upon the "Inexhaustible Bottle," inasmuch as the Wizard's Bottle will not only be inexhaustible, but will change its contents—ad infinitum, at the word of command, producing Soda Water, Buttermilk, Epsom Salts, Port, Sherry, Brandy, Gin, Rum, Whisky, Noyeau, &c., &c.; and finally proving to be filled with Pocket Handkerchiefs perfectly dry, and occupying the whole space when tightly packed.

ACT VI.

HALF-AN-HOUR WITH THE SPIRITS

Or, AN EXPOSE OF SPIRIT-RAPPING.

Introducing the Spirit-Rapping Table and the Tocsin of the Invisibles.

ACT VII.

LE LIVRE DES RECUEILS CHOISIS;

Or, PUCK'S OWN POCKET BOOK,

WITH PUCK HIMSELF WITHIN IT.

Typifying the Evening's Entertainment in the production of the very voluminous from a small volume, in the extraction of magnitude out of minuteness, in developing bulk where no space appears for its existence, in discovering odd things in odd places, and in bringing forth unexpected wonders from the most unlikely place for them to be found.

Revival, in an Improved Form, of the Astounding Novelty which startled London 10 Years ago—The

GREAT GUN TRICK!

Or, THE SECRET OF INVULNERABILITY.

Anybody will be allowed to FIRE AT THE WIZARD, and 100 Guineas will be paid to the Sportsman who succeeds in aiming a bullet at him which he fails to catch.

AN INTERVAL OF FIFTEEN MINUTES.

PART II.

ACT VIII.

THE AQUA-AVIAL PARADOX.

Exemplifying the power of producing Animated Nature from Fire and Water only, and the possibility of eliciting from the simplest elements the most complex forms of Ornithological existence.

ACT IX.

GRAND MYSTIC AMALGAM;

In which the Property of the Wizard's Patrons will undergo some strange Metamorphosis, and, amongst others, their Handkerchiefs become transformed into the

FLAGS OF VICTORY!

THE BANNERS OF ENGLAND, FRANCE, TURKEY & SARDINIA

ACT X.

THE ENCHANTED CHAIR OF COMUS,

In which he who seats himself will be under the Magic Spell, and appear to the Audience, under circumstances least expected, in a position, peculiar as perplexing.

ACT XI.

The MYSTERY of the CHARMED CHEST;

Or, THE NUCLEUS OF THE NIGHT'S WONDERS!

To comprehend which, the Audience will have the goodness to observe, in an earlier part of the Evening, the Chest suspended, like Mahommed's Coffin, in mid-air, into which all things will travel, and out of which all will be produced.

ACT XII.

HOMOLOGICAL EVAPORATION; Or, The SHORTEST ROUTE TO THE ANTIPODES.

Illustrating the easiest mode of ridding ourselves of a troublesome Friend and the advantages of the newly-discovered dia-terrestrial passage from the Western to the Eastern Hemisphere.

using ideas of other magicians, and it was unnecessary for him to make such extravagant claims. What he did for magic was to form a new conception of what a magic show should be. His definition of a magician was an actor playing the part of a legendary man of power. He also simplified his stage equipment so that the few appurtenances he did use seemed to be devoid of the deception that older apparatus so obviously had. It is true that steps in this direction had been made by earlier magicians, particularly Frikell.

Robert Houdin was born and raised in France, and played most of his life in that country. As a boy he was apprenticed to a clock-maker, and became skilled in that work. This had not a little to do with his later success as a magician, for it not only made him conscious of the value of small details—indispensable in magic—, but his training in the trade gave him the skill necessary to construct his own intricate apparatus.

Without doubt Houdin's greatest contribution to magic was his books; in them he gave magicians a professional attitude, and for the first time set down rules for being a magician. All the earlier books had merely given meager details of how tricks were done. Houdin was the first to describe how to do them; there is an enormous difference between knowing how a trick works and knowing how to do it.

Houdin had a most interesting life, but the two best stories are of how he got into magic and of his last work as a magician. While still a young apprentice watch-maker, he took a stage to go home for a holiday. He was ill, and had a high fever, and accidentally, owing to his weak condition, he fell out of the stage unknown to the driver. Soon after his fall, Torrini, a wagon-show magician, drove along the road, and found the boy. He picked him up, took him in the wagon, and nursed him back to health. During his convalescence he taught Houdin the skill of a magician, and Houdin acted as Torrini's assistant for some time in return for his kindness. Although after leaving the wagon-show Houdin again worked as a watch-maker, he gave it up for magic as soon as he felt his skill in the art would permit it.

After Houdin had retired, the government of France asked him to use his talent to strengthen the country's position in Algeria, where the natives had never ceased making trouble from the day the French took possession of the country. The Algerians were encouraged in this by their priest-magicians, who claimed that their magic coupled with continuous fighting would shortly drive the French from the country. The French government sent Houdin to Algeria to prove to the people that the French had, not only

more powerful armies, but magicians who were infinitely better than native ones. For his work there Houdin devised several special feats, which to the natives seemed possible only if Houdin could perform true miracles. His trip as special Ambassador Magician was completely successful; when the native magicians were shown to have inferior miracles, the Algerians gave up their continual fighting.

We American magicians owe it to an Englishman known as Robert Heller that audiences of cultured American theater-goers care for magic. He was responsible for simplifying magic in this country, and was the first to bring it recognition as an art. Heller was an accomplished musician, and often appeared as a pianist in recitals. His regular performances consisted of exceptionally dexterous magic, a piano concert, second sight, and sometimes an amusing puppet-show.

While he was a skilful magician, his delightful manner and the witty and gentlemanly conversation with which he accompanied his magic were quite as enjoyable as the tricks themselves.

Second sight, which had been featured in Europe by Robert Houdin, among others, was the feat of having a blindfolded assistant on the stage describe any article shown to Heller while passing among the audience. It was called second sight because what the magician was able to see the second person by some unknown method seemed also to see. It is still performed by magicians, and is a trick as one would naturally suppose. But it is very effective and extremely mystifying all the same. It was not his own mystery; for Heller was not an inventive magician, but was content with being a superb entertainer.

Although, as aforementioned, Heller was an Englishman, he had never made a success of magic until he came to America, and even here he abandoned it for a while to return to music. After he had made his name he returned to England, where he was known as an American. It is hardly ever possible to be certain of the nationality of a magician. There have been Englishmen known as Germans, a German thought to be Spanish, and so the confusion goes until we find an Italian taken for an American Indian, and a Hollander whom everyone understands to be Chinese. Even in their nationality magicians are men of mystery.

One of Heller's most impressive feats was copied from the program of Robert Houdin, and was called "The Orange Tree." At the beginning of this trick a handkerchief bor-

MONS^r

ROBERT-HOUDIN,

THE CELEBRATED

PRESTIDIGITATEUR

AND

FRENCH CONJURER,

WILL CONTINUE HIS ORIGINAL

EXPERIMENTS

AND WONDERS OF

NATURAL MAGIC,

As Invented by him, and Performed for Ten Consecutive Seasons at his Théâtre
Palais Royal, Paris, under the title of

"SÉANCES FANTASTIQUES."

THESE EXTRAORDINARY REPRESENTATIONS WILL BE CONTINUED

AT. THE ABOVE THEATRE,

FOR A LIMITED NUMBER OF REPRESENTATIONS,

EVERY

TUESDAY AND THURSDAY EVENING,

At Half-past Eight o'Clock,

AND A

DAY PERFORMANCE

ON

WEDNESDAY & SATURDAY MORNINGS

Commencing at Half-past Two o'Clock.

PROGRAMME.

PREMIÈRE PARTIE.	DEUXIÈME PARTIE.
LE SOLDAT INTRÉPIDE.	LES BOULES DE CRISTAL.
LES CARTES ANIMÉES.	GRANDE SERIE DE TOURS D'ADRESSE.
L'ORANGER MYSTERIEUX.	LA NAISSANCE DES FLEURS.
LA LORGNETTE DE MÉPHISTOPHELES.	LA TRANSPOSITION INSTANTANÉE.
LES TOURTERELLES.	LA PLUIE D'OR.
LE COFFRE DE CRISTAL.	LA GUIRLANDE ENCHANTÉE.
LE VASE OU LE GENIE DES ROSES.	SURPRISES POUR LES DAMES.

TROISIEME PARTIE.

LE MERVEILLEUX BOWL DE PUNCH.
LE COMBAT DES ELEMENTS.
LE PETIT TOM ENSORCELLÉ.

STALLS, 7s.   BOXES, 4s.   PIT, 2s.   GALLERY, 1s.
PRIVATE BOXES, £1 1s., £1 11s. 6d., & £2 2s.

OPERETTA HOUSE, WATERLOO PLACE.

FIRST ENTIRE CHANGE OF PROGRAMME,

TO-NIGHT, AND EVERY EVENING AT 8.

Illuminated Matinees every WEDNESDAY and SATURDAY at 3, specially recommended to Ladies, Children, Private Schools, and Suburban Residents.

FIFTH WEEK'S DIGNIFIED SUCCESS! GENUINE APPLAUSE!! LAUGHTER PREDOMINANT!!! MYSTERY TRIUMPHANT!!!!

EXTRAORDINARY AND SUSTAINED POPULARITY IN EDINBURGH OF

HELLER'S WONDERS

As Originated, Invented, and Performed only by

MR. ROBERT HELLER,

The Unrivalled American Entertainer, assisted by his Sister,

MISS HAIDEE HELLER,

And introduced with astounding success in England, America, California, Australia, New Zealand, India, Ceylon, China, and Java.

Fauteuils (2 front rows), 4s.; Reserved Carpeted Stalls (6 rows), 3s.; Front Area, 2s.; Area, 1s.; Gallery, 6d.
Children and Schools Half-price, except Gallery.
Places may be secured in advance at Messrs WOOD and Co.'s. Music Sellers, George Street.

That the Public may be satisfied of the Truth of every Announcement, Mr. Heller's Portfolio of Press Opinions and Travels can always be inspected on application.

SECOND MONSTRE PROGRAMME OF WONDERS, COMMENCING APRIL 26, 1875.

Part 1.—PRESTIDIGITATION and NECROMANCY.

1.—The Desicated Canaries.
2.—Fortunes and Misfortunes of a Handkerchief.
3.—The Witches' Pole.
4.—Ravel. (A French Clown.)
5.—A Curious Omelet.
6.—The Money Hunt.

Part 2.—MUSIC.

Mr. HELLER will perform three Brilliant Solos on a Magnificent Grand Pianoforte, by BLUTHNER, of Leipsic, specially selected by the eminent piano manufacturer, WADDINGTON, YORK, and purchased by W. J. BULLOCK, expressly for HELLER's Wonders.
I.—MAZURKA, "JOSEPHINE."—*Heller.*   II.—CAPRICE, "Il Trovatore."—*Heller.*
III.—BALLAD, "AULD ROBIN GRAY," performed on the Orgue Melodique.—*Heller.*

Part 3.—MYSTERY.

The PHENOMENON of SUPERNATURAL VISION, as exemplified by

MISS HAIDEE HELLER,

Introducing the Marvellous SEALED PACKET MYSTERY for the first time in Scotland.

Part 4.—INSTRUCTIVE.

Mr. HELLER will conclude his Programme with a novel and interesting performance, entitled

PARLOR MAGIC.

W. J. BULLOCK, Responsible Manager.

·31·

rowed from a spectator vanished. Then Heller called attention to a small potted tree. At his order the tree began to bud. The blossoms grew, and fell to the floor, and the tree started to bear fruit. All the full-grown oranges but one were plucked, and passed to the audience. The topmost orange left on the tree suddenly split open, and from the inside flew two butterflies bearing the spectator's handkerchief.

The late Professor Brander Matthews, who had made a life-long study of conjuring and conjurers, told me that Heller was the most entertaining of all the magicians. Dr. Matthews knew Heller intimately, and even invented a trick for Heller's program. The trick was an addition to another effect, and took only a second to show, but it impressed Heller's audiences. Heller had caused two cards to rise from the deck while he stood quite apart; both cards were those previously selected by the audience. The third card which rose was not the one chosen (and here was Dr. Matthews' addition), but at Heller's order it instantly changed to the selected card.

The name of Herrmann is one of the best known in magic, and this only partly because the family produced several magicians. The first was Samuel Herrmann, a German physician who now and again abandoned pills in order to travel about as a magician. His conjuring met with success, and he gave a number of royal performances from France to Turkey. The eldest and youngest of his sixteen children were boys. Compars, or Carl, Herrmann, was the first born. He found magic interesting, and became a leading magician. The youngest child, Alexander, while still a boy became his brother's assistant, and later started out with a show of his own. Both men gave their shows in America, but the one best remembered was Alexander, or, as he was better known, Herrmann The Great.

The small picture on this page is of Carl Herrmann. The larger picture is of Alexander, who demonstrated to American magicians the value of clever pantomime, of

proper presentation of his effects, and above all of bright, witty and adult patter. Besides helping magicians by his example, Herrmann the Great with his culture and gentlemanly manners convinced the world that a magician was an artist rather than an unholy vagabond.

One of the tricks featured by Herrmann, the gentleman in the picture, was that of catching on a plate marked bullets shot at him from standard army rifles. The feat was

always sensational, and perhaps particularly so because it was really dangerous. It was an old trick even in Herrmann's time, and many magicians had been injured or killed while attempting it. One of Herrmann's assistants who later himself became a favorite performer in England met his death by the failure of this mystery. His name was Campbell, and he came from northern New York State. He later called himself Robinson, and still later while in England he was known by a Chinese name, and thought to be Chinese. So men of magic change their names and color with the ease with which they transform roses to rings.

While Herrmann The Great was better known in America, Carl was more famous in Europe, although each had crossed the ocean many times. In fact when Alexander first appeared in the United States he was brought over by his elder brother, and they toured together as they had previously done in Europe. There is a story that they finally divided the world between them, Carl to remain chief magician in the Eastern Hemisphere while Alexander would conquer the Western. Carl perhaps was not so skilful as his younger brother, or maybe found more worthy competitors in Europe, for he never stood pre-eminent as did Alexander in both North and South America.

Upon his death the widow of Herrmann The Great sent for his nephew Leon to appear with her and continue the Herrmann show. He had neither the personality nor the skill his uncles had, but bore a great facial resemblance to them and is therefore often confused with one or other. Madame Herrmann afterward carried on alone for about twenty-five years.

Alexander Herrmann was a magician at all times, and on the slightest pretext would

perform what seemed to be extemporaneous miracles. Probably no other magician in America has ever so constantly and completely played the role of friendly sorcerer.

It seems strange that one of the most prominent men ever to be in magic could do hardly any legerdemain at all. In that he was the exact opposite of Herrmann, and yet perhaps no man ever exerted a greater influence in magic. He was John Nevil Maskelyne, an Englishman, and he, like Robert Houdin, began as a skilled watch-maker.

MONDAY, Aug. 21, 1876.

EVERY EVENING at 8, and WEDNESDAY AND SATURDAY AFTERNOONS at 2.

FOR THIS WEEK ONLY!

The world-renowned and unapproachable Prestidigitateur,

PROF. A. HERRMANN

—— IN A ——

NEW WORLD OF MAGIC AND LEGERDEMAIN!

PROGRAMME.
PART FIRST.

1. Flying Cards.
2. Wonderful Mind-Reading of Cards.
3. Magic Cigar Case.
4. All Nations in one Bottle.
5. Invisible Knots.
6. Mysterious Rabbit.
7. Arabian Trick.
8. Coffin Du Gran Mogul.

PART SECOND.

Exposure of the Wonderful Spiritual Seance!

PART THIRD.

1. Indian Foulard.
2. Enchanted Flowers.
3. Sympathetic Doves.
4. Solomon's Letter.
5. Flying Watches.
6. Four in One.
7. Comic Scenes.
8. Wonder of the Nineteenth Century.

MASKELYNE & COOKE,
THE
ROYAL ILLUSIONISTS.

SIXTH YEAR IN LONDON.

Tuesday, Thursday and Saturday Afternoons at Three, and every Evening at Eight.

PART I.

OVERTURE (GRAND PIANO) MR. CHARLES MELLON

The Piano was made specially for the Entertainment by Messrs. J. & J. HOPKINSON, of 235, Regent Street.

MR. J. N. MASKELYNE, will open the programme with his original feats of

PLATE SPINNING

FOLLOWED BY

JAPANESE TOP SPINNING

PSYCHO AND ZOE

THE TWIN AUTOMATIC MYSTERIES.

FANFARE!

MR. MASKELYNE'S FIRST MUSICAL AUTOMATON.

LABIAL!

MR. MASKELYNE'S SECOND MUSICAL AUTOMATON.

PIANO SOLO ... ... MR CHAS. MELLON.

Illusory Sketch, entitled

ELIXIR VITÆ!

Dr. de Botus ... Mr MASKELYNE
Gloucestershire Farmer ... Mr COOKE

MUSICAL INTERLUDE.

Grand Piano - Mr. C. MELLON.

Exposition of Spiritualism so-called,

LIGHT AND DARK SEANCE
EXTRAORDINARY,

Including the Appearance of the spirit-form of

JOHN KING.

AND

Floating Mr. Cooke from the Stage to the Ceiling in the Centre of the Hall,

AND OTHER

Mysterious Manifestations!

Private Boxes, from £57 — 10s.
Fauteuils, 5s. Stalls, 3s. Area, 2s. Balcony, 1s.
Seats can be booked at any time during the day, at the Box Offic free of charge.

Places can also be secured at the following Opera Ticket Agents:—Bond Street—Mitchell's Royal Library, Lacon & Ollier, Bubb, Ollivier, Chappell. Cornhill—Hays City Box Office. Cheapside—Keith & Prowse. Regent Street—S. Hays. St. James's Street—Harrison's Library.

Messrs. MASKELYNE & COOKE had the distinguished honour of a Royal Command to perform before H.R.H the Prince of Wales, at Sandringham, on Monday, January 11th, 1875.

Price 6d.—A Book containing a full description of the Entertainment and brief Biography of Mr MASKELYNE can be had in the Hall.
Price 1s.—Spiritualism (Rape for the Rappers), being a short account of the Rise and Progress of Modern Spiritualism, with exposures of the frauds of so-called Spirit Media by JOHN NEVIL MASKELYNE can also be obtained of the attendants

111. C

Maskelyne's start on the stage was due to an accident. The mishap occurred during the demonstration of supposed spirit manifestation by the notorious Davenport Brothers, and it permitted Maskelyne to catch them in trickery. He denounced them publicly at once, but some in the audience thought him the cheat, and wished to believe in the Davenports. In order to clear himself he offered to duplicate the performance as soon as he had had the essential rehearsals. He gave the show with the help of a friend, George A. Cooke. They were asked to repeat the demonstration, and shortly gave up all former connections to tour professionally with their show.

For eight years Maskelyne and Cooke took their show touring before they finally decided to settle in London. During these years they made many additions to their entertainment. Maskelyne perfected himself with a juggling feat of spinning plates which he had seen Blitz perform. (Antonio Blitz, for many years a favorite in America, always featured the spinning plates). Utilizing his watch-maker's training Maskelyne also built several automatons—mechanical human images so designed that they not only moved but seemed capable of reason.

When Maskelyne and his friend and business associate took a London theater for three months, little did they or the public dream of their remaining at this theater continuously for thirty years. But they did, only to move finally to a theater specially built by Maskelyne, where the shows continued for twenty more. The show was carried on by Maskelyne, his sons, and grandsons for more than fifty thousand performances.

Maskelyne's part, besides his juggling and automatons, (one of which he is shown demonstrating) consisted in building and presenting large mechanical effects and in managing his theater. Great as was his personal contribution, he stands out even more as a patron of magic, for he engaged and presented at his entertainments literally hundreds of magicians. Many of these performers were really started on their road to fame by Maskelyne.

Cooke having died just before the move to the new theatre, Maskelyne took David Devant into partnership. London theater-goers were just as loyal to Maskelyne and Devant as they had been to Maskelyne and Cooke, and well they might be, for Devant was (he is now retired) England's leading magician. The small portrait (p. 40) is of David Devant.

Maskelyne, who is shown with one of his automaton figures, made his greatest contribution to magic by showing magicians the advantage of working together on a friendly and

mutually helpful basis. I believe it is not too much to suggest that Maskelyne's example of the value of cooperation among magicians encouraged the magicians to form their own organization. There are now many societies of magicians throughout the world, devoted to helping magicians and magic.

Joseph Buatier was one of the many magicians who at one time appeared at Maskelyne's. It seems quite certain that he was born in France, although I have a program in which he called himself a Belgian, and have heard other nationalities claim him also. In later life he called himself Buatier de Kolta, and by this name he was best known. His portrait on the previous page shows him rather severe looking, but on the stage he was kind and jovial.

He was a skilful performer, and presented his magic with great artistry, but he is remembered by magicians of today because of his inventive abilities. There is probably no magician now working who does not at sometime during his performance make use of at least one of de Kolta's mechanical contributions. In fact Buatier de Kolta's large and spectacular effects have made the fame and fortune of a score of magicians. Perhaps the most sensational was the one for which he brought upon the stage a small cube, each side of which was about as long as a cigar-box. He announced to the public that he carried his wife inside the box. In order to prove his statement he set the box upon a low table, where it at once grew to be as large as a packing case. He carefully lifted this large box from the table to show Mrs. de Kolta sitting inside. All this happened before the spectators' eyes.

De Kolta's big magic was ingenious and a large step in advance of the mysteries which had previously been shown, but his inventions of smaller tricks have been more helpful to later magicians. One of the best of his tricks is that in which a canary bird, cage and all, dissolves into nothingness, the instant it is tossed into the air. He conceived this amazing mystery more than sixty years ago, and since then at least a hundred prominent magicians have made canaries and their cages disappear countless thousands of times.

Another magician who by his inventive bent advanced magic was Johann N. Hofzinser, probably the best of all the Austrian magicians. But while de Kolta originated large as well as small magic, Hofzinser's fame rests principally on the ingenious small appurtenances and manipulative methods he devised.

Perhaps eighty per cent of a magic show's success rests upon the way the tricks are pre-

sented and the manner in which the magician gets the audience to respond. The psychology of presentation and the psychology of deception are both extremely important in magic. Ten per cent of a mystery is usually due to sleight of hand, and another ten per cent to some carefully hidden mechanical device.

In all probability John William Sargent did more research than any other magician into the mental processes of audiences. He was the first magician, at least in America, to correlate the work of the academic psychologists with the magician's wide but indefinite knowledge of the psychology of deception. He formulated many rules whereby magicians could know more definitely the responses they might expect from audiences faced with any given trick.

He also studied the timing of magic. Timing is the all-important art of the right emphasis at the right moment. Before Sargent made his study the timing and misdirection, which is the magicians' term for the psychology of deception, were worked out in a hit-or-miss way for each new trick. When one magician found a way which proved successful, other magicians would mimic his every intonation and gesture. Sargent proved that it was possible to have presentations apparently quite unlike, and yet based on the same rules.

I had the honor to have John William Sargent as my master in magic, and he was very particular that I should never present any magic as he presented it. He once told me, "If you do your magic your own way you may, or may not, become a skilful John Mulholland, while if you copy me you will always be merely an imitation of Sargent." He insisted that I study the performances of all the magicians I could see; at each performance I must consider why the trick had been good or bad, why the audience reacted as it did, and whether the magician was able to make the audience like what he showed them. All magic depends on clearly understandable facts, and if a trick is not successful it means that the magician ignored or did not know one of the rules.

As I look at the photograph of Mr. Sargent in his characteristic pose with one hand held behind while he gestures with the other, I recall his repeated advice, "John, remember, it is what the audience believe you to have done which matters, not what you actually did." If a magician properly suggests his miracles by a few highlights the spectators from their own imagination obligingly fill in all the half-tones. The conjurer's illusions depend on psychological conditions, and if he uses these and is clever enough to make his false steps seem logical, the impossible may be achieved with the greatest of ease.

The first really great American magician was Harry Keller, who was born in Erie, Pennsylvania. Owing to the similarity between his name and Heller's, he altered the spelling to avoid confustion. As Kellar the Magician he was known and loved by audiences from New York to San Francisco.

Kellar did not have the flashing wit of Herrmann, but he was a much more careful performer. In fact he showed American magicians by his example the perfection which meticulous attention to detail can bring. He made no move while on the stage—not even the blinking of an eye—which was not the result of careful study and rehearsal. If genius is the infinite capacity for taking pains, he was a true genius. Other magicians may have had more innate ability, but none gave a finer show.

Kellar I knew well. In fact beginning with Mr. Sargent, I know, or have known, intimately the rest of the magicians I shall mention in these pages. I also knew John Nevil Maskelyne's sons, and know his living grandsons. Herrmann the Great's widow I also knew for many years. Kellar I first met while I was still a small boy, and a very thrilled boy, for he showed me many of his tricks. Perhaps one of the reasons Kellar was always so friendly to boys was that he recalled the kindness of The Fakir of Ava, a magician with whom he traveled as assistant from the time he was twelve until he was eighteen.

The photograph shows Kellar with Ching Ling Foo. Ching was the first of the really great Chinese magicians to come to America. Each man had the highest regard for the ability and skill of the other; they were always exceedingly proud of this picture.

Robert Houdin said that the three essentials in magic were: first, practice; second, practice; third, practice. Ching Ling Foo went even further than this; he declared that no one could really be a skilled magician with less than forty years of constant practice. Old Ching in his stage performance, like Kellar, was precise in every action. Not by a hair nor a split second did his motions vary.

As is so frequently true with magic, what he did quite under one's nose was the most impressive. Extraordinary as was Ching's stage magic, where by the wave of a silk scarf be pulled from the air a number of huge filled bowls and a boy, his feats done close by —such as mending a torn slip of paper, or picking cherries from the air in the dead of winter—were even more perplexing. They were perfectly done.

Houdini, like Kellar, and for that matter practically all other magicians who have attained any great skill, began his magic as a boy. He travelled with a circus, he appeared with carnivals and small touring companies, and all the while he gained experience and kept everlastingly practicing. Houdini's photograph on the next page shows an intelligent face full of determination; the one on the page following shows Houdini, hanging by his heels, making an escape from a straitjacket.

Houdini was known to millions of people the world over as the "Elusive American,"

because he specialized in the branch of magic which permitted him to escape from whatever box or contrivance he was put into. His ability to get out of even the most ingeniously constructed restraints was mainly due to his having a greater knowledge of the various methods of confinement than did anyone who tried to hold him. But he made audiences interested in his efforts because of his superb showmanship. The definition of showmanship Webster's gives is adeptly exhibiting things to advantage. He made of showmanship a fine art, and he demonstrated its inestimable value not only to magicians but to the theater world. It is not too much to say that he was the greatest showman America has known. His showman's instinct led him to show feats which challenged and defied the public.

He was a great reader, and no detail of magic or the lives of magicians was too small to concern him. He knew more about the subject than anyone I have ever known. He was the authority on locks, ropes and knots, and anything which might bear on his escape work in the smallest way.

So magic developed with one man adding psychological principles and another improving mechanics. One magician showed the value of advertising, others of humor, deportment, attention to detail, and above all of showmanship. To the magician who will take the trouble to delve into it, magic today offers a well-rounded whole built from crude beginnings by many hands. To be a good magician you have only to apply that knowledge.

Present-Day Mystifiers

MODERN MAGIC MAY BE SAID to have started approximately with this century. Some of the men who have been leaders, however, were famous before that time. Others, now of the past, notably Houdini, made their reputation after 1900. It is impossible to say that those men who appeared before a certain year were old-fashioned and those who came after were modern. It cannot be emphasized too strongly that skill is not a matter of period but of individuals.

Servais LeRoy, who had international fame even in the last century, is still one of the most inventive of living magicians. He has devised many small bits of magic and numerous illusions. Originally an illusion was something based entirely on illusory optical principles, but today *illusion* is the magician's term for those effects, regardless of principle, in which men or women, lions or elephants, are used rather than cards or coins, handkerchiefs or rabbits. LeRoy apart from being original is a dextrous and delightful entertainer.

Just before the start of this century Servais LeRoy was one of the magicians to form a partnership called "The Triple Alliance." Frederick Eugene Powell, a polished performer, was one of the partners, and the third was Imro Fox, a humorous magician. Powell, still active, has toured America and as far away as Australia with his magic, and has been a magician for more than fifty years. Fox and his comedy and magic, until his death in 1910, were familiar to audiences in both America and Europe. LeRoy is a Belgian, Fox was a German, and Powell, the American in "The Triple Alliance."

LeRoy, Fox and Powell appeared together and separately with their own acts in their show. It can easily be imagined that when these three were doing magic simultaneously, the audience simply abandoned itself to amazement. At times they left the stage; one went to the orchestra, one to the balcony, and one to the gallery to take coins from spectators' ears and playing cards from their pockets. For once the gallery patrons were really considered part of the audience. Among the tricks the three wizards showed together was the production of large flags of all nations. The photograph shows them at this trick: Powell, Fox and LeRoy, from left to right.

Several years after "The Triple Alliance" dissolved, Harry Kellar had with him, during his last tour, a young magician named Howard Thurston whom he announced as his successor.

Thurston had been one of the American magicians who had specialized in a particular branch of magic. In his act he used only cards. He made cards appear at his finger-tips, and a moment later caused them to return to the air from which they had come. He made cards change their color or size, or become transformed to different cards at command. He made cards float in air. Not only did he cause those cards which he chose to rise unaided from the deck and soar above his head, but he permitted a spectator to call out the name of the card. Once named, the card would free itself from the pack, and ascend or descend at the spectator's order. Thurston and his fifty-three cardboard assistants were a sensation in England as well as America.

After several successful years Thurston decided to tour the world. Of course card tricks alone, while spectacular in a short act, were not enough for a full evening's entertainment, so he put together a more elaborate show. His tour was profitable; and Kellar asked Thurston to return and join his company.

For over twenty years Thurston travelled about the United States with an entire evening's show. To those feats which he had taken over from Kellar, he added others from time to time. He appeared in the best theaters in the largest cities, and was always beloved by audiences. Recently he has shortened his program in order to appear as the stage attraction in large moving-picture theatres.

Another specialist who began about the same time as Thurston is T. Nelson Downs, known as the King of Koins. The title was bestowed upon him by some press-agent who was more alliterative than literate. During his act coins were made to do things which they never did at any other time. The air of the stage seemed thick with coins which only Downs could see, and which only he could pluck. He filled his hat with silver pieces which were nowhere, and yet everywhere about the brilliantly lighted stage. All this magic was produced by dextrous fingers and good acting. Although Downs still practices,

he has been retired for many years. He came from a town in Iowa, and gave up the stage to return to that town when he had saved the amount he had decided upon. His picture appears on this page.

Howard Thurston is shown performing the illusion of sawing a woman in half which he has featured for several years. The marvel of sawing directly through a human body must be accredited to Horace Goldin.

Goldin has for years presented a show consisting mainly of illusions. He does his magic with a speed and dash which have never been equalled by another performer. To watch an act done quickly and yet with certainty adds interest, although it is not necessarily better than magic done slowly. Even though his main interest is in large spectacular illusions, Goldin is a superb manipulative conjurer and an accomplished showman.

To me one of Goldin's most amazing feats is an apparently simple thing done with large handkerchiefs. The handkerchiefs with knot upon knot are tied end to end by the spectators. Goldin tosses them on a chair, waves his hands over them, wiggles his fingers in the air and picks up the handkerchiefs quite separate; the knots have vanished completely. Even though it is no great trick, he presents it ably and artistically. I particularly like the way the photographer has caught Goldin at the start of this trick in the picture on page 59. At times Goldin has appeared in a variety bill; often he gives a complete show. Owing to the success of his European tour it is more than five years since he has appeared in America.

The illusion performed by Goldin which appeals most to me is called "from a film to life." It is a whimsical little play which takes place partly in moving pictures thrown on a screen, and partly on the stage. Goldin appears at one moment on the stage, and the

next walks right into the picture. He seems to be able to alter his substantial body to a screen picture and back at will. In the picture Goldin meets an attractive girl and suggests to her that she walk out of the picture with him. He leaves, and returns to the stage, but she appears afraid, so he asks her to take his hand, and he helps her to step right off the screen. The moment she does so she is transformed into a flesh-and-blood reality.

Although as in the past each magician does some magic which the others do not do, many tricks and illusions will be found time and time again on the programs of various magicians. Some of these effects are modern versions of old magic, and others are bought from the inventors by the performers using them. Infrequently we also find some magician appropriating for his show without permission the effect of another performer. Besides inventing tricks, buying them or getting them in trade, magicians add to their programs magic described in privately circulated books or periodicals. There are a number of such magazines published throughout the world from here to India. Most of these papers are published by societies of magicians for their members. The first magicians' magazine was published in England in 1792. The second was brought out in Italy about a hundred years later. The oldest still continuing publication (*The Sphinx,* an independent magazine having its office in New York City) was started in 1902.

A few months after *The Sphinx* began publication The Society of American Magicians was organized; it still thrives. Shortly afterwards The British Magical Society was formed; it too flourishes today. Since that time magicians have organized from Brazil to China. There are few countries not having a club of mystifiers, for magicians are clannish, and like to mix with their own kind. The private shows of these societies are most interesting, and no better audience for magic exists than a group of magicians.

Magic is truly international in its appeal, and we magicians find that the mysteries which confound the New Yorkers will be liked quite as much by audiences in Peking or Paris, Bombay or Berlin. Since this is true, magicians are apt to travel extensively.

My friend Carter, Nicola, and The Great Raymond with their big fine shows are quite as well known in Europe and the Orient as in America. Sometimes magicians continue to play in their own countries as did Kassner the German and as does Birch the American. Long Tack Sam and Chefalo are truly international; the changes in their patter from one language to another are almost as amazing as their magic. Long, the Chinese, even speaks Yiddish; he is quite as skilled in European magic as in his native kind, and the reverse is true of Levante the Australian. Magic today is the most international of all the arts.

It is not the purpose of this story to list the names of all those modern magicians who give elaborate shows, but among the best-known are Harry Rouclere, Dante, LaFollette, Dr. Caligari, S. S. Henry, and the late Maro. Henry just returned from an oriental tour; immediately before he planned to sail home from China he had a tragic loss. He was appearing in a native theater, and shortly after the last performance, a fire broke out in the

building and destroyed a large part of his scenery and equipment. What little the fire did not touch the firemen either pulled apart or ruined with water. As if that were not enough the river steamer he and his company engaged to take them back to the coast caught fire, and although everyone escaped serious injury, they lost most of their personal property. Being a magician is not all spotlight and applause.

One of the younger of the big show magicians is Harry Blackstone, and as a newspaper printed today said, he "is really a great magician". I have always enjoyed his performance, but choose as his chief effects his smallest magic. His illusion of causing a horse to disappear I like as well as the other major mysteries, but two little tricks are personal masterpieces. In one he borrows a handkerchief; and by tying a knot in one corner he makes it alive. It writhes and wriggles and hops and jumps. It follows all instructions until the obviously meaningless knot is untied, when it is again merely a handkerchief. The other favorite the photographer has caught Blackstone performing. He fills a glass with milk. By a few passes with his hands toward the glass he makes glass as well as milk wander floating all about the stage and even over the heads of the audience. Blackstone, like Horace Goldin and Alexander Herrmann, is quite as prepared and delighted to mystify one off the stage as on.

Many magicians in preparing themselves to confute the spectator's reason at any time have studied all angles of mystifying. Naturally the successful ones become authorities on deceptive methods. Magic is a delightful art, and it is little wonder that magicians dislike the people who claim to be spirit mediums, and who use trickery to dupe rather than entertain. Anderson, Maskelyne, Kellar, Houdini and countless other magicians have worked diligently to show the public that these self-styled mediums depend upon chicanery.

One of the best-informed men on the trickery of the dark seance room is Elmer P. Ransom. He has toured America many times during nearly sixty years in vaudeville and with his own show. He is a convincing, clever and delightful magician. As a young man Ransom was engaged to introduce Margaret Fox during the tour she made admitting her supposed spirit work was all imposture. Margaret Fox and her sister Katie may really be called the founders of the modern spiritistic-seance fad. The principal fraud these women perpetrated was given the name of "spirit raps." The knocking, supposedly produced by ghostly hands, was in reality brought about by the Fox sisters' adroit manipulation of their toes. During this tour in 1888 she not only demonstrated her ability to make these raps, but she also taught Ransom the method. During this tour she gave to the press a statement in which she as one of the instigators denounced spiritism as a fraud and a deception. "It is a branch of legerdemain," she said, "but it has to be closely studied to gain perfection." The strangest thing of all is that even today, in spite of their tricks' being known, in spite of the complete confession of Margaret Fox, millions of people claim to believe in the ghostly power of the Fox sisters. Today's trickster

mediums, like the magicians of centuries before, traffic in the credulity and ignorance of their followers.

Following the lead of Margaret and Katie Fox the Davenport Brothers began their cabinet "manifestations." They planned their work more for stage presentation than had the Fox sisters. As has been said before, Anderson and Maskelyne both exposed the Davenports' fakery, and Robert Houdin also denounced them. Kellar had traveled with the men, and knew and could perform all their feats, and Ira Davenport, after the death of his brother William, taught the methods to Houdini.

The Davenports specialized in escaping from the rope binding with which they were tied to prove (they claimed) they had no connection with what later took place. Ransom, those previously named, and others could do, and regularly did, the same feat in order to prove that spirit aid was unnecessary. The spiritistic tricksters continued to add to their repertoire. They made writing appear on slates, bells ring, and tables rise. They caused ghostly forms to appear, and ghostly voices to talk. Of course much of what is done by these "mediums" takes place in the dark; in the words of Ira Davenport, "Strange how people imagine things in the dark." Not all the belief in ghost return is due to gullibility, for the cheats of some of these fakers are clever, and expertly done. It is too bad that they do not use their skill to entertain rather than to defraud.

The message signed "Margaret Fox" on the slate which Ransom is holding was produced by a simple and mystifying trick without the aid of a darkened room.

Knowing how easily people can be fooled, and realizing their extreme eagerness to credit some supernatural agency with their mystification, writers three hundred and fifty years ago wrote assurances that all was due to "juggling knacks." Again and again since then other writers have likewise ascribed it all to superstitious beliefs or trickery. It is amazing that literally millions of people still believe in the same old nonsense. Each time the number begins to wane, a few new terms are coined, and the horde flocks back to be swindled again.

Of course, as in all other branches of trickery, new ideas have come out in the psychic world, but for the most part these are needless, since people will continue to buy the same old psychic gold bricks as long as they are offered for sale.

The tragically amusing part of it all is that in their eagerness for self-delusion believers in the occult often tell us that in magic we are really aided by spirits, for our work is possible only with their help. Our noisy protestations to the contrary are ascribed frequently to malice, but usually to ignorance. I claim that Houdini knew more about the magic he performed than did anyone else, and most certainly more than one who could do no part of it. I feel quite certain I know the methods of my own mysteries. After sixty years of practice and successful presentation is it not fantastic to suppose that Elmer P. Ransom does not know how his magic is performed? And yet people still bother him

Among the magicians doing acts in vaudeville are Chris Charlton, The Great Leon, Carl Rosini, Henry Huber, Edward Victor, Cortini, Nixon, and Okito and Hardeen, mentioned before. Their magic is quite different, and runs all the way from Charlton, who causes his wife to dissolve into nothingness in plain view of the audience, to Nixon, who pours water into a tub, and pours out ducks instead.

Magicians are frequently asked how many different feats there are in magic. I have never heard of any magician who dared to estimate. Once Mora, an unbelievably skilful sleight-of-hand man, and I began early one morning to do card tricks for one another. Each feat one showed would remind the other of a different mystery. The cards were passed back and forth until eleven that night. Even at meals one was performing while the other ate. At the end, to the best of our recollection, no trick had been repeated. This had not been done as a stunt at all; it was merely that once started on card tricks we kept on until other engagements separated us. We had not only not covered the subject, but had hardly scratched the surface of the knowledge of this one kind of magic. Several years ago I had a shorter session in Vienna with Larette, a superb manipulator. That time our tricks were done with coins, and while some were known to us both, several I did he had not heard of before, and he did many which I had never seen. There are literally hundreds of thousands of different tricks in magic. I have a library of thirty-five hundred books on the subject, but I know that there are many thousand other tricks never disclosed in books.

To return to our story, one of the younger American vaudeville magicians is Jack Gwynne. He is shown holding the silk scarf from which he has shaken the nine bowls filled with water. Gwynne got the idea from this amazing production from the Chinese, but his method is quite different from the old celestial technique. Gwynne is extremely popular with audiences and with his brother magicians. He is genial, and his act is delightful. Although, besides feats of dexterity, he presents several illusions, he uses no bulky apparatus. In fact the small space into which his equipment can be packed is almost as marvelous as the magic itself. In my opinion the elmination of bulky paraphernalia makes his show most modern. Automatic magic must be discarded because of the mechanical marvels of every day life. Magic began as a manipulative art, but magicians, like the rest of the world, became enamored of machinery. Various mechanisms were designed to produce the effects which had formerly been possible only by years of practice. A school of button-pressers evolved, and has largely passed again. Although mechanical contrivances may still play a subtle, minor part in magic, great skill is now essential in their use. Gwynne has been willing to work literally years to perfect an act which takes but fifteen minutes to show.

The polished sleight-of-hand of modern magicians must be quite as exactly done as

the playing of music by an accomplished musician. Everyone realizes that in piano music each note on the printed score means a definite movement of a particular finger at a precise instant. There are often thousands of notes in one musical selection, and memorizing the notes is merely part of the musician's task. In magic the part each finger plays in a particular trick is as definitely prescribed as in any piece of music. As there is no score for magic, memorizing the thousand or more movements for each trick can be

done only by intensive practice. Magicians do not have ten-finger exercises like the pianists, for no exercise has been devised which will develop the muscles used in magic. It is necessary to go on rehearsing each trick until the particular hand muscles used are under perfect control.

Somewhat like vaudeville shows are the Lyceum or Chautauqua performances, but in these the variety comes not in each show, but in the different entertainments, on successive days. Magic is quite regularly included in the series because it is one of the most delightful amusements. Edwin Brush, The Jewell Brothers, Germain, Ducrot, Paul Fleming and Al Baker, all formerly specialized in this branch of show business. Today perhaps the best known are Eugene Laurant and Walter E. Floyd.

At the beginning, specialization in magic, as we know it today, was a purely American movement. The specialized acts of Thurston, Downs and Houdini have already been mentioned. Another magician who has featured modern magic—magic without paraphernalia—is Nate Leipzig. Leipzig became famous at about the same time as the others, and was also a sensation in England.

Leipzig's act is purely manipulative: he features card tricks. He has been starred in vaudeville theaters from Cleveland to Cape Town. After his initial appearance in London, the Magic Circle, for the first time, struck a gold medal, which they presented him for the excellence of his work. He was honored by many command performances; the Empress Eugenie wrote in her diary, later published, a most complimentary notice of his appearance before her.

Leipzig's manipulative magic is superbly dextrous and confounding; without any display of skill or effort, he demonstrates miracles with cards. In one of his favorite effects,

he begins by allowing two cards to be chosen freely by members of the audience. These cards are replaced in the deck, the deck is thoroughly mixed, and wrapped in a piece of newspaper. Leipzig takes the small bundle, and with a table-knife cuts through the paper. The knife is left between two cards. Leipzig, as in the picture, tears open the newspaper to show that the cards on both sides of the knife are the ones chosen. Reason tells us that this is impossible, but in magic the impossible is the rule.

On page 68 is a picture of Gus Fowler, a brilliant English magician, who modestly ascribes the idea of his novel act to having seen Leipzig. Fowler made up his mind that it was utterly impossible to better Leipzig's technique, so he felt compelled to devise an entirely new type of magic. His entire act is done with watches and clocks. These time-pieces appear, disappear, and multiply in a most amusing way. At the close of his act, Fowler opens an opera hat, and takes out a stage-full of alarm clocks, the bells ringing full blast. Fowler developed the entire act himself, and I know of no one in magic with a more ingenious or fertile brain. He too has played the furthest corners of the world.

When I last visited Fowler in his home in Birmingham, he took me to his workshop to show me his latest clock trick. In this effect he claps his hands, and a giant alarm clock the size of an automobile instantly appears on the stage. Naturally a clock of that size has a bell in proportion, and the bell made trouble; the first time the trick was rehearsed the fire department came rushing up to put out the fire.

Fowler's sleight-of-hand is very fine, which means, as mentioned before, that his fingers have mastered thousands of moves. Beside the detail in the hand manipulation there is more detail work to be learned in the presentation of the tricks. To bring forth the dozens of clocks from the empty hat Fowler not only has to be skilled in the sleight-of-hand of getting the clocks into the hat unnoticed, but must also recall where each one is hidden, and by his studied smooth manner get to that spot naturally. Kellar told me that he had an uncomfortably difficult time during one performance because two tables were placed six steps apart instead of five. All his patter and actions were planned for the space of time it took to take five steps; the extra step made him seem awkward, and made the audience suspicious.

The details of presentation must be outlined so that they are psychologically sound and convincing, and so that everything looks natural and easy. Ade Duval, whose best-known act is built around one trick with a myriad of detail, is an excellent example of a master of small points. I had watched his act many times from an orchestra seat and marveled at the mastery of his work. When at his invitation I stood on the side of the stage with him during a performance, I was astounded to notice that I, even though I am a magician, had previously missed literally hundreds of points.

Duval's feature trick is done with the small tube he is shown holding. He begins by showing this to be merely an empty metal tube. He then closes both ends with paper held in place

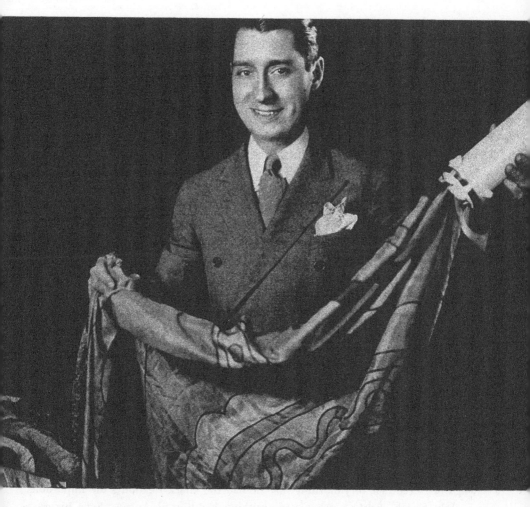

by rings which fit tightly on the tube. He shines a light through the paper to show the tube still empty. Then, breaking the paper on one end, he begins to pull yard after yard of brilliantly colored silk from the tube. He continues to do this, quite as rapidly as it is possible to move, for some five or six minutes. Once the act is over and the curtain has fallen, assistants with large clothes-baskets clear the stage.

Duval, having started this act, devoted himself to a serious study of types of silk, the best way of keeping them, and even found it necessary to develop his own process for dyeing and painting silks. In short he is an authority on silk, because it is necessary for his magic. Fowler has a very wide knowledge of clocks and watches, and no one has ever had a more exhaustive knowledge of locks than did Houdini. The one thing an audience will not countenance is for a magician to fail in his trick. In order to minimize the chance of failure magicians study every angle of their work.

After all the details for doing the magic are learned, the magician must add the acting necessary for the presentation. As Robert Houdin pointed out, the magician must first of all be an actor. At first thought it would seem quite easy to act the part of oneself, and ordinarily it would present little difficulty, though even then, owing to the fact that actions on the stage must be exaggerated, a person cannot merely be natural. In magic the acting becomes more difficult because the performer must make the unusual actions required by the trick seem most ordinary.

Earle Larimore, well-known for his fine work on the legitimate stage, does magic as a hobby. He told me recently, "While pantomime is a difficult but fundamental requisite for acting it becomes doubly difficult in the magician's art owing to the added manipulation necessary." Knowing that pantomime in magic besides building the characterization has to shield the method of the trick, we realize at once how important—and difficult—it is.

Any number of magicians, as competent actors, have found it advantageous to leave magic. One of them is Fred Keating. He is now featured in Hollywood. He had appeared in leading roles in several Broadway plays before he went into moving pictures. While Keating's magic is very skilful he was always noted for the clever delivery of his patter and for his acting. The part he played as a magician was that of a suave young man to whom a miracle was of small moment, though rather amusing. He gave the impression of having discovered that very morning that he had the knack for doing the impossible, as one might find he could touch his toes without bending his knees. Even his most startling effect would be nonchalantly and almost casually shown. The photographer has caught him sitting on top of a stool, amused by your mystification as he tells you the name of the card you had in mind.

Cardini is another magician whose acting is outstanding. His act is an example of the highest type of magician's pantomime. Cardini, whose picture appears on page 75, seems to find his magic every bit as comfounding as does his audience. His magic is extremely

simple—to watch. All he does is to find in the air a dozen or so packs of cards, a carton of lighted cigarettes, a score of billiard balls, and perhaps a filled cocktail glass or two. One is convinced by his pantomime (for he never speaks) that he is quite at a loss to find the air so filled. Cardini uses no apparatus, no elaborate setting, but super-marvels occur.

Cardini's trick of finding the air full of burning cigarettes and Keating's presentation of the DeKolta disappearing bird and cage have each been described by newspaper writers as the best feat in magic. Is there a best trick? I doubt it. It is true that some magic tricks get talked about more than others, but that is usually because they are more sensational or because the effects are simple enough to describe. But magic to be magic must be mystifying, and the method of performance will always be a source of wonder.

I have had as many as a dozen different people come to me after a performance, and each mention a different trick as the best in my show. It is likely that each possessed some special knowledge, and the trick which ventured into his field appealed most to him. A person who frequently plays cards will find a card trick much more interesting than will a man to whom cards are so many pieces of pasteboard. One with mechanical knowledge will prefer a trick which defies the laws of mechanics. The professional man likes best the tricks which he feels challenge his reason rather than his eyesight. As long as tastes differ so radically there can be no best trick; after all, it is the performance rather than the trick. The feature effect in one magician's program may be the least interesting in another's, and probably there is no trick which will fit into the style of all magicians. It may be an excellent effect, and yet be as unsuitable as a dwarf's suit for a giant.

Then if there can be no best trick who is the best magician? Jack Gwynne announces he is the world's second best magician, for he says everyone else seems to be the world's best, and he does not want to be lost in the crowd. It is true that theater press-agents, always fond of superlatives, usually announce the magician at their theaters as the "world's best." I have announcements by one publicity man who made the same statement about six different magicians in one season.

Magicians, as I have pointed out, present very different performances. Was Houdini's escape from a nailed box a better performance than Thurston's causing a girl to float in air? They cannot be compared. It is quite possible to say that no one presented the box escape better than Houdini, and that no one shows the levitation as does Thurston. But even in the same type of magic there are difficulties in making comparisons. I have always said that Leipzig is the best sleight-of-hand performer in the world, and yet I consider that Cardini has the best sleight-of-hand act on the stage today. I do not consider this at all contradictory, for I am not comparing Leipzig's exquisite skill with Cardini's flawless act. A man who uses patter in his act may or may not give a better show than one who does not talk.

The very fact that I have mentioned certain magicians in my story means that I con-

sidered them the best in their particular branches of mystification. There are thousands of magicians performing in America today, and many thousands more in other countries. I have not named any of the large number of magicians who appear privately, because most of them are known only locally. Nevertheless some of these men will compare favorably with the more famous stage performers. The best Chinese magic I ever saw was done by a young, unknown magician appearing at a cheap fair near Peking. The best man with East Indian magic is the hotel proprietor at Agra. His name is Edwin Hotz, and he isn't an Indian. There are many thousand skilled amateurs in magic, which may seem strange

considering the amount of work needed before it can be done; but magic is so fascinating that the work is not arduous. To name the best performer for each trick would mean that all the tricks and almost all the magicians would be mentioned. There is hardly any magician who does not do some trick better than anyone else.

Even though the one best magician and the one best trick cannot be named, I want to give the program for my ideal show. I realize that this show is only a dream, for besides the prohibitive cost there is never a time when all the magicians would be in one city at once. Thurston would make the girl float in air. Goldin would change back and forth from a screen shadow to a real man. Blackstone would get into a box, an assistant would shoot a pistol, show the box empty, and turn out to be Blackstone himself. Coins and watches and cigarettes would mysteriously appear at the finger-tips of Downs, Fowler and Cardini. Charlton would make his assistant vanish—poof! and Duval would take silks from the inexhaustible tube. Birch would make a pony disappear, and Long Tack Sam would produce a huge bowl of water. And there would be Keating and Gwynne, and the show would go on and on. I would like to sell programs for that show.

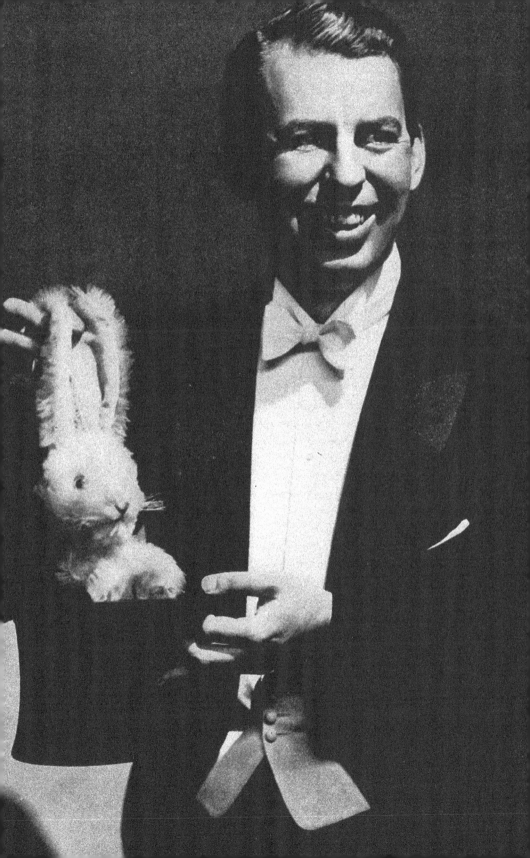

(Being afraid that Mr. Mullholland would not do justice to one of the finest modern magicians, the publishers conclude the book with the following note by another hand.)

"Pharaoh would have rejoiced in so good a tricker," said Alexander Woollcott. "One of the soundest and most learned authorities on the history of magic," said Lowell Thomas over the radio. "He is one of the greatest masters of magic in our time, a trained scholar as well as a superb practitioner of the art," said John Erskine.

These are rare tributes to a single magician. Some of the greatest conjurers have barely been able to sign their names; most of the sound magical historians are content to watch others do tricks; but the man in the pictures (besides being all three men himself) has a New York apartment overflowing about equally with magic tricks, rare magic books, and famous magicians. He could paper a wall with membership scrolls in foreign magical societies; he runs one of the oddest of all magazines, the magicians' trade journal (*The Sphinx*) ; he has written books. You guessed it—this book is his latest. The suave gentleman withdrawing the rabbit from the hat, Ching Ling Foo, Mohammed Bakhsh the Hindu, all are disguises of John Mulholland, who was a magician at five, a teacher in his twenties, and the leading lecturer on magic and occultism by the time he was thirty. He has probably had more command performances before royalty than any living American magician. He also probably knows more about the technical side of magic, and has introduced a number of European and Oriental tricks into this country.

Mulholland is ingenious, skilful, and a superb showman; but the most striking feature of his work is its perfect effortlessness. Watching his performance you would scarcely dream that this big, friendly man had any uncommon skill except as a host. In private he can do the most astonishing juggling flourishes with coins and cards, but on the stage he would never give himself away so crassly. People who have the privilege of sitting up all night watching Mulholland at home declare that his trick of changing quarters into half-dollars while somebody holds his wrists is perfect. Others, who have seen him only on the stage, claim that his Hindu trick of growing flowers in full view is not merely better than the Indian original, but better than anything else even Mulholland can do. It is certain that the half-dollar trick will fool anybody; and John Mulholland (whose knowledge of Oriental magic is unequalled in the United States) has indeed progressed so far as an Eastern magician that he not only does their tricks but borrows their gestures, their very faces. If it's magic, he does it; if it's a magician, he knows him; if it's been done, he can explain it (but won't).

There is probably no one so active in the world's magical organizations. He is the only non-native member of some foreign societies; the only honorary member of others; the only foreign officer of the British Magical Society. The magician who has never heard of John Mulholland must be an ignorant conjurer indeed. One is tempted to say the same of the general public, though as Mulholland has visited only 41 countries there may be people who actually have never heard the name. There are a number of fortune-tellers and other fakers who wish they never had, but that is another story, and belongs not to the history of magic but to the trials of being a swindler.

We hope some day to read his autobiography, which in itself would be a history of modern magic, and an entertaining travel book—to make no mention of his friends among the famous.

The End.